Think Like a Baby

....

Think
Like a Baby

33 Simple Research Experiments You Can Do at Home to Better Understand Your Child's Developing Mind

AMBER ANKOWSKI, PhD, and ANDY ANKOWSKI

(The Doctor and the Dad)

CHICAGO
REVIEW
PRESS

Published by Chicago Review Press Incorporated
814 North Franklin Street
Chicago, Illinois 60610

ISBN 978-1-61373-063-8

Library of Congress Cataloging-in-Publication Data
Ankowski, Amber.
  Think like a baby : 33 simple research experiments you can do at home to better understand your child's developing mind / Amber Ankowski and Andy Ankowski.
     pages cm
  Summary: "This book gives parents tremendous insight into their children's physical, cognitive, language, and social development Think Like a Baby features 33 lab-tested research experiments parents can easily re-create at home to give them tremendous insight into their children's physical, cognitive, language, and social development. Presented in a lighthearted, entertaining, yet authoritative manner, each experiment is followed by a discussion of its practical implications for parents—why to bring more than one toy to a restaurant, why not to overuse a baby walker, which baby gadgets to buy (and not to buy), surefire tactics for keeping keys and cell phones out of baby's mouth, how to get her to be perfectly happy eating just half of her dessert, and much more. With this book, amazed parents won't just read about how their children are developing; why they behave as they do; and how to be a great, effective parent, they will actually see it all happening while interacting and having fun with their child at the same time"— Provided by publisher.
  Includes bibliographical references and index.
  ISBN 978-1-61373-063-8 (paperback)
  1. Infants—Development. 2. Infant psychology. 3. Parent and infant. 4. Parenting. I. Ankowski, Andy. II. Title.

  HQ774.A68 2015
  305.232—dc23

                              2014039013

Cover and interior design: Sarah Olson
Cover photo: dolgachov/Bigstock.com
Interior illustrations: Jim Spence

Printed in the United States of America
5 4 3 2 1

For Sammy and Freddy,
our beloved little guinea pigs.

Contents

Introduction

•••

No matter how many baby books you read, videos you watch, or classes you attend before your child is born, at some point after the little one arrives, you're bound to face that moment.

You know the one.

First, you completely forget how to breathe. Then your eyes grow so big that your forehead disappears. Your heart starts beating in your ears, two of your hairs immediately turn gray, and all you can do is ask yourself, "What the heck am I supposed to do now?"

When *that moment* happens to you (and if it hasn't already, trust us—it will), it's easy to start thinking that maybe you just don't have what it takes to make it as a parent. After all, you don't *really* know the best way to take care of your kid. You can't see what's going on inside her adorable little baby brain. And if it weren't for that color-changing strip thingy, you wouldn't even be able to tell what was going on inside her diaper half the time.

But why is understanding our children so difficult? Is there any way for us to get better at it? And is it even possible to become a new parent *without* feeling the panic-stricken need to revert to the fetal position ourselves?

That's exactly what this book—and the academic research studies it's based on—can help you find out.

Psychologists who study how the human mind thinks, learns, and develops over time know that if parents can get inside their kids' heads, they'll have a much better chance of determining what it is they need—and the best ways to give it to them. They also know that figuring out what kids are thinking isn't as simple as it is with adults. After all, newborns haven't learned how to speak our language yet, so we can't just ask them what they're thinking. And even when toddlers do start talking, we tend to spend less time discussing the intricacies of their thought processes and more time trying to decipher all their adorable mispronunciations. *Mimi*? That's *Mommy. Cumpootoob*? That's *computer*, of course.

So how *have* these researchers come to understand what's going on inside a child's mind? The answer comes right out of your middle school science textbook: experiments.

For those of you whose memory about things you learned way back when you were twelve is a bit fuzzy, here's a quick refresher on the subject. In a nutshell, an experiment is a carefully designed test meant to support or disprove a hypothesis. That hypothesis thing? It's basically your best guess as to what you *think* will happen when you perform your experiment. So to use an example that appears in lots of seventh graders' science fair projects every year, suppose you start wondering about how plants grow. You hypothesize, or guess, that giving plants fertilizer will make them grow faster. So as an experiment, you plant two identical seeds in two identical pots, put them in the same window, and give them the same amount of water every day. The only difference is that you give one of the plants fertilizer as well. Over the next few weeks, you'll be able to observe and measure how quickly each plant grows, which should tell you whether your hypothesis was right or wrong.

(Spoiler alert: the one with fertilizer grows faster. Duh.)

Experiments have helped people make all sorts of important discoveries over time, like the cure for polio, the secret of space travel, and the surprising fact that fried chicken and waffles taste awesome together.

They've also taught us just about everything we know in the field of child development. Each day, thousands of researchers from around the world are creating, performing, and evaluating results from experiments that give us insight into the way children think. Although these experiments often involve elaborately constructed laboratory equipment and complicated statistical analyses, the basic ideas behind them are actually pretty simple.

That's the main reason this book exists: to take a bunch of classic, proven child development experiments that highly trained researchers have learned from over the course of many years, and then simplify them, so that *you* can use them to learn about your own kids. Experimentation can teach you the smartest ways to talk to your child, the times when plunking your kids in front of the TV is OK, and which popular baby gadgets you really ought to avoid. The experiments in this book are quick and easy activities you can do with your child, yet they provide tremendous insight into what's going on inside your kid's brain at different points of development. After all, they're the same experiments the experts have used. It's just now, we've taken them out of the lab and brought them into your home.

For you skeptical parents out there who at this very moment are thinking something like, "I don't know about this book. I mean, performing scientific experiments on my sweet, little, adorable monkey-poo just seems *wrong*," we have a couple comments especially for you. First of all, "monkey-poo" is a supercute nickname. Keep using that as long as your kid lets you. (Las Vegas oddsmakers are setting the over-under line at age nine and a half.) And second, performing experiments on your child isn't wrong at all—it's one of the most natural things in the world. In fact, when you really think about raising a kid, the whole darn thing is one great big experiment.

For example:

You might notice that, although he's perfect in just about every other way, little Junior tends to wake the whole house screaming bloody murder every forty-five minutes all night long. So you perform a little experiment, shelling out fifty bucks on a blanket specially designed to prevent your newborn from moving his limbs even a fraction of an inch. And lo and behold, turning him into a tightly wrapped medieval torture burrito works! At least for a couple of months. Then you discover that he won't even go to sleep until he's been bounced and rocked and walked around in circles until *you're* the one who's practically passed out from exhaustion. So you run some other tests, comparing your hand-me-down antique rocking chair with the newfangled glider that got such great online reviews to exercise balls of varying circumferences, attempting to determine which one will get you out of that nursery and back in front of the TV the fastest (with your back thrown out the least).

Each time you solve one scientific mystery, the next one presents itself. How do you get him to eat his infant mush cereal (then later, his vegetables)? Why won't he try harder on his algebra homework? When's he going to find a nice girl and settle down already? Why don't he and the kids ever call me on my futuristic, 3-D holographic videophone? Doesn't he know I want to see my grandchildren?

The experiments in this book may not give you every single answer you're looking for, but they *will* help you understand what's going on inside your kid's cranium better than any textbook ever could. Rather than simply reading about how your child thinks or what his abilities should be like at a particular age, you will actually be able to see it for yourself.

And speaking of doing things for yourself, that's the other great thing about the experiments you'll find in this book. Sure they're here to help your child, but they're also here to help *you*. Because let's face it, as a parent, you need all the help you can get. Rest assured that behind their insanely cute exteriors, your children are constantly plotting against you—scheming new ways to test their limits, exploit your weaknesses, and drink more chocolate milk than any pint-sized human rightly should. Today they're refusing to take a nap, and tomorrow they'll be forcing you into a nursing home against your will. And if you're not careful, you'll have lost every battle in between, too.

That's why these experiments—and the lessons you learn from them—are so important. With the proper insight into your kid's mind, you can discover ways to regain the upper hand and solidify your position as master of the family. Read on, and you'll learn how you can cut your kids' dessert expenses in half, get your cell phone out of their hands whenever you want to, and even catch a few extra ZZs while you're watching them. The more you know about the way your kids think, the better prepared you'll be to defend yourself against them when they inevitably attempt to crush your very soul.

Because when it comes right down to it, being a parent is tough. It's intimidating. And it's scary. But the fact that you're panicking about it means that you care. And to be a truly amazing parent, that may be all you really need.

Well, that and this book, of course.

About the Doctor and the Dad

When you're making the weighty decision to turn your babies into lab rats, you don't want to do it alone. Fortunately, this book is filled with advice from two competent and compassionate guides ready to assist you in your studies.

Amber Ankowski is a doctor of developmental psychology with a PhD from the University of California, Los Angeles. As a researcher, she has performed experiments on hundreds of kids of all ages, focusing her studies primarily in the field of language and cognitive development. As a professor, she shares this knowledge about how humans learn best in undergraduate and graduate-level courses full of preschool teachers, psychology researchers, and other child development professionals. In addition to instructing her students on the theoretical aspects of child development, Amber also likes to impart practical tips about raising children that will make her students better parents, aunts, uncles, grandparents, and role models for the kids in their lives.

Andy Ankowski is Amber's husband. As an advertising copywriter and creative director, he wears T-shirts to work and writes commercials all day. He's never actually studied psychology or child development, but he hears lots of Amber's stories on the subject over dinner. And then he makes jokes about them. That's pretty much what he does in this book, too.

Together, Amber and Andy are hunkered down in the trenches of intergenerational warfare every day, parenting just like you. With a daughter who decided by age two that every directive given to her was merely the start of a negotiation (actual, oft-repeated conversation: "OK, Sweetie. You can stay up for three more minutes." "No, *all* the minutes."), and a son who at nine months old learned to thwart diaper changing attempts by contorting his body into an unwieldy, poop-covered pretzel, they've certainly had their hands full. But they've also found that conducting experiments like these is a great way to understand their kids a little bit better—and to have a lot of fun with them too.

About the Experiments

Here's some important stuff to keep in mind before you put on your white lab coat and start poking your kids with a stick: First, don't poke your kids with a stick. None of our experiments tell you to do that. Where did you even get that idea anyway? Second, you don't need to wear a white lab coat to do these experiments. But you should. It's frisky and fun, and if you don't mind us saying so, it looks damn good on you.

Third (and the first real, nonjoke thing in this section), the experiments in this book are meant to be fun ways to learn about your kids. They cannot be used to assess children's development. They won't tell you if your child is a genius or has a developmental delay. If your child's behavior doesn't match an experiment's predicted results, that's no reason to freak out. If you're already freaking out right now and you haven't even done a single experiment yet, go open a bottle of wine. Pour yourself a glass.

We'll wait.

So like we were saying, there are lots of reasons your results for any of the experiments could vary. One thing to remember is that the age ranges included in this book are all *approximate*. Individual children develop at drastically different rates, so it would be totally normal to find that your child exhibits a described behavior a few months before or after the predicted time frame. Also, don't be worried if your child's behavior *never* matches the predicted results. These predictions are taken from studies that compile the average results from many, many children. Just because researchers have learned that, on average, children performed in the ways described in this book, it doesn't mean all individual children will perform in exactly the same way.

Also, don't forget that your kid *is a kid*. And kids' behavior can be pretty unpredictable. Some days your child will draw pictures that make you think he's the next Monet, and other days he'll just make wet farts in his underpants. Your child's performance in these experiments, just like most other aspects of his behavior, can and will continually fluctuate.

Finally, if you're still looking for an explanation as to why an experiment didn't quite work for you, let's face it, you probably flubbed up the directions. It's not like you've been getting a ton of sleep lately. Plus you're drunk. Seriously, put down the wine already.

The First
Year

Congratulations, parents! You are about to have more responsibilities, federal tax deductions, and mounds of garbage coming out of your household than you ever thought possible. You also have lots to learn about the new little life-form you've just brought into the world. So as soon as the nursery is set up, it's time to turn it into a science lab, and let the experimenting begin!

The first year of your child's life is a time of tremendous change. Your baby begins the year as a tiny person with little control over his own body, and ends it as a slightly less tiny person who can move himself around way more than you're comfortable with. He goes from crying as an unconscious, automatic reflex to crying as a way to blatantly manipulate you, and from sticking everything he sees into his mouth to vehemently refusing to eat anything green.

With your baby growing and changing so fast, it can be hard to make sense of it all.

1

That's why doing experiments this year will be so useful. They can help you understand your baby's behavior by explaining how your child's motor skills develop, what he perceives with his senses both in and out of the womb, and how he quickly begins to learn all kinds of things about his world.

But the most remarkable thing you'll learn about your baby is how amazingly smart he already is. He may look like he's doing nothing a lot of the time, but he is in fact soaking up his surroundings and learning from them all the time. As a result, he already has way more knowledge hidden beneath the surface than you are likely to suspect.

And that's what this year's collection of experiments is all about—showing you all of the incredible things your baby knows at a time when he couldn't even begin to tell you himself.

Tiny Tunes

Think you have to wait until your baby is actually *born* to start running tests on it? Think again. Your first opportunity to turn your child into your own personal guinea pig comes well before your due date.

This experiment is intended to give you your very first glimpse into how your adorable little fetus's memory works. It can also give you a chance to start the parent-child bonding process early.

Because who really wants to wait until the kid's a full-fledged *infant* to do that?

Age	Ability Tested
3rd trimester–1 month	Memory

What You Need

☞ a "baby bump"

☞ your favorite song or children's book

☞ complete indifference toward strangers who look at you like you're a crazy person

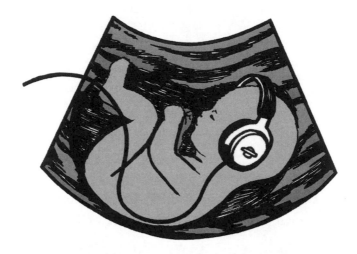

How It Works

1. During the last trimester of your pregnancy, read your favorite children's book out loud or croon your favorite song right at that increasingly bulging baby belly.

2. Repeat daily or as often as the mood strikes until your beautiful baby is born.

3. After the big day has come, unswaddle your baby, lay her down on a flat surface, and read the book or sing the song again.

4. Watch and see what your child does.

So you're getting ready to have a baby. Congratulations! Fifteen years from now, your child isn't going to listen to a single word you say. But right now, while that little angel is still trapped inside Mommy's uterus, you have a captive audience. It doesn't matter what you say or how off-key you sing, your kid has nothing else to do these days but listen to you. And listening—and remembering—is exactly what she's doing.

It's true! By the third trimester, your baby's ears and other sensory organs have developed enough to allow her to hear sounds coming from outside her pregnant mommy's body. But in addition to simply *hearing* these sounds as they are happening, researchers performing experiments similar to this one have shown that newborn babies will actually *remember* them later as well. In these experiments, pregnant women were asked to read the same story to their babies every day for the last six weeks of their pregnancies. After the babies were born, the mothers read either the familiar story or a new story to their babies. The babies reacted differently depending on which one they heard!

So if you have a song you plan to sing with your baby or a special story you anticipate reading to her, don't wait until after she's born— you can start right now. Choose quiet times, use a loud, clear voice, and be sure to repeat the process many times. It might feel a little awkward to be reading a book out loud to an invisible baby or singing childhood songs to yourself (especially if the only times you remember to try this experiment are while you're shopping for groceries or standing in line at the DMV), but your baby *will* be listening, and she will remember what she hears. It's pretty amazing to think that by doing something as simple as talking to your unborn baby, you can create a shared experience that will begin to bond parent and child before you two ever lay eyes on one another.

You may feel your baby reacting to your chosen song or story while you're still pregnant, becoming more active and kicking or rolling around in the womb. Later, after your baby is born, you will be able to *see* her reaction when you sing the song again. Does she get extra active and kick around as you sing? When you start reading your story, does she suck faster on her pacifier or stop fussing to listen?

In our case, our daughter's reaction was unmistakable—even before she was born. When we were expecting our first baby, Andy would often sing the song "Mrs. Train" by the band They Might Be Giants to our little one, and we would watch as Amber's baby belly would bob around to the sound of the music. When our due date passed and Amber hadn't yet begun labor, our OB had us come in frequently for nonstress tests.

During these tests we would sit in a quiet room for fifteen minutes or so while the baby's heartbeat was recorded in the form of jagged little lines printing out onto a never-ending spool of paper.

During one of these tests, we decided to entertain ourselves by having Andy sing the now-familiar song to the baby. As soon as he started, the baby's heart rate—which had been hovering steadily between 130 and 140 beats per minute—shot all the way up to 165. The chart rolling out of the monitor morphed from gently rolling hills into a series of extreme peaks, cliffs, and drop-offs. We were alarmed. Andy stopped singing. We felt like we had done something bad and we were going to get in trouble. When the doctor walked in to read the machine's output, we held our breaths. But she said that the baby's heartbeat looked great, "especially this part," pointing to the spikes Andy had helped create when he sang the song. The doctor explained that she liked to see changes in the baby's heart rate like that because it indicated that the baby was being active. When the doctor left, Andy resumed the song and the baby danced along to it (or so we can only assume based on the pointy heart rate chart and the colossal kicks Amber was feeling).

Later, when our daughter was about two weeks old, we laid her on the couch and Andy sang the familiar song again. She became immediately alert and excited, kicking and flailing her little arms around. We were able to see firsthand how she must have been reacting in the womb.

Most of us don't really think about unborn babies as real people. We wonder what gender they are and what we might name them, but we don't think of them as actual human beings that have already begun experiencing the world. But a baby in the womb is busy using her senses and practicing things that she will do after she is born. She drinks, pees, hiccups, and cries, all the while listening to the sounds around her.

By twenty-four weeks of gestation, her hearing system is so well developed that she can experience the sounds of the world from inside the womb. She hears cars go by as you walk down the street, she hears your favorite music play on the radio, she hears you snore as you sleep at night, and she hears you talk every day. That's why you can soothe your baby so much quicker than anyone else—she was born already knowing the sound of your voice! She also recognizes the sounds of her native language. A baby who has heard English in the womb prefers to hear the sounds of English over the sounds of other languages. In that way, the baby's auditory experience in the womb primes her for learning language.

Tips to Help Your Child

If you're really into music, you may already have plans for treating your baby to some of the true classics—Mozart, the Beatles, NKOTB. But when it comes to helping your child's development, it turns out that *what* music you choose to play for her isn't nearly as important as *how* you choose to play it.

You can either expose your child to music passively (by playing your favorite tunes on the stereo while you play, read, eat, or generally go about your day) or actively (by interacting with each other and the music via singing, dancing, or playing musical instruments to the beat). And babies get a lot more out of music when you take the latter approach.

Researchers investigating the effect of music on two- to six-month-olds found that babies exposed to regular sessions of *active* musical interaction—like going to a structured music class or doing music-class-like activities at home—reap a variety of benefits. Not only can they better distinguish different musical tones, but they also tend to start using more gestures earlier, which is an important preverbal method of communication. Active musical interaction benefits the parent-child relationship as well. After all, how could you *not* be better friends with someone after an afternoon of singing, dancing, and playing together!

Tips to Help Yourself

Concerned your kid's going to be a picky eater a few months down the road? You may be able to put the kibosh on that right now. In addition to hearing, babies also use their other senses in the womb, including taste. Flavors from the food a mother eats will actually season her amniotic fluid. And since a not-yet-born baby is frequently swallowing the fluid around her, she gets a good sample of the foods her mother eats.

Researchers discovered this after instructing one group of pregnant women to drink carrot juice every day during their last trimester of pregnancy and a second group of women to drink only water. The results of the study showed that the women who drank carrot juice during their pregnancies had babies who enjoyed carrots more when they were introduced as baby food.

That's why it's important to remember that the foods you eat while pregnant can actually help to shape your child's future food preferences. (Since diet affects the taste of breast milk too, the same thing applies while you're breast-feeding.) If you want your children to eat their vegetables at age six, you'd be doing everyone a favor by eating them yourself right now. And if you are trying to decide whether or not to breast-feed after the baby comes, one thing you may want to consider is the fact that, in general, breast-fed babies tend to accept new foods more readily than their formula-fed peers, because breast-fed babies are exposed to a greater variety of flavors. Although a mother's diet is full of the various foods a baby will later eat, formula is stable in flavor and does not contain any previews of flavors to come.

Full disclosure: our kids turned out to be complete and utter chocolate fiends. We are not at all surprised by that.

Because the foods you eat during pregnancy and lactation are so influential to your baby, it's extra important to eat more healthy foods during those stages of your child's development. Not only are they better for you and your baby, but tasting them now may also help your baby to like them more later. It's never too early to create healthy habits!

A Face Only a Baby Could Love

Ah! The new baby has finally arrived! And by now you've discovered many of the fun and exciting things that come along with it: sleep deprivation, an increased tolerance for wearing clothing covered in other people's bodily fluids, and, of course, lots and lots of visitors wanting to see the baby.

And what do all of these well-wishers do when they show up? They peer over the side of the cradle at the tiny new addition to the family—and make the stupidest faces imaginable at it.

This experiment will show you how to turn this weird phenomenon that every newborn on earth goes through into a learning experience—both for you and for your kid!

Age	Abilities Tested
0–3 weeks	Learning, Social Development

What You Need
- ☞ an awake, alert, full-bellied, calm, contented, not-crying-or-about-to-cry-or-just-finished-crying baby (that rare and elusive creature you may have heard about in legend)
- ☞ the ability to control your own face

How It Works

1. Position yourself in front of your baby so that he has the best possible view of your face—he should be looking at you straight on, at a close distance, in good lighting. (Keep in mind that his eyesight is not too great yet.)

2. Slowly protrude your tongue out of your mouth, then pull it back in, over and over for about twenty seconds or so. If you were raised to believe that sticking one's tongue out is not behavior befitting a well-mannered member of society like yourself (perhaps by a wealthy blue blood or a humorless British headmistress), you can just open and close your mouth instead.

3. For the *next* twenty seconds, look at your baby without doing anything with your tongue or mouth.

4. Repeat steps 2 and 3 for as long as it's fun for you and your baby.

If everything went according to plan, you probably noticed that during the times you were sticking your tongue out or opening your mouth, your baby was more likely to do the same. Pretty cool, huh? Your little one was rudely thrust out of his cozy cocoon only a few days ago, and to the untrained eye he appears to be no more than a grunting, sleepy, little ball of deliciously squishy flesh. But in actuality, he's already prepared to play his first game of Simon Says.

Your newborn came into the world with well-developed senses that he practiced using while inside the womb. And now that he's here, he's ready to immediately begin deciphering all the sensory input that the blooming, buzzing, bustling world throws at him. As a parent, you are a great big part of that input. That's why your baby will look for you when you walk across the room, turn when he hears your voice, respond to your scent and to your touch, and plant his slobbery little taste buds all over you whenever you give him the chance. Observing you is one of the very first ways your new baby learns. And imitating you—as this experiment demonstrates—is one of the most basic ways he shows you what he knows.

Your baby applies this incredible ability to observe and mimic you to learn lots of things, from the relatively minor trick of sticking out his tongue to ultimately more complex and useful tasks like feeding himself and telling a good story over the dinner table.

His ability to imitate actions quickly develops, so that by six weeks old, your baby can already *remember* and *reproduce* facial expressions. Using the same procedure as the one you used in this experiment, researchers found that six-week-old babies not only imitate facial expressions while they're watching them, but they will also continue to repeat those facial expressions over the next twenty-four hours. So try this again in a few weeks and you will observe not only your child's impressive ability to learn in the moment but also his even more impressive ability to remember what he's learned over time.

The moral of the story? Don't underestimate your kid. It's easy to assume your baby is too little to understand the things you do and say, but the fact is he's absorbing way more than you think. Your child was born with a foundation for learning, and he's ready to build on it. So make sure you're ready to start teaching!

Tips to Help Your Child

Kids learn all kinds of things through imitation, including how to treat other people. That's why it's extremely important that you provide positive relationship models for your child to imitate.

It's no secret that having a baby puts a lot of stress on a marriage. You have way more to do, you get a lot less sleep, and you have to rely on each other all the time. In a situation like this, conflict is bound to flare up. But once you have kids, it's more important than ever that you deal with conflicts effectively. In part because kids are such natural imitators, children who witness more marital conflict at home tend to be more aggressive themselves. They also exhibit frequent attention problems, difficulty regulating their emotions, higher-than-average levels of depression and anxiety, greater health problems, worse grades in school, and lower IQs.

By only six months old, babies already exhibit negative behavioral responses (looking distressed or crying) and physiological responses (including changes in heart rate, blood pressure, and the production of stress hormones) when exposed to marital conflict.

Here are a few simple tips for maintaining a positive, strong relationship:

* ***Be nice to each other.*** Being pleasant and doing nice things for each other throughout the day can help to keep a relationship healthy—the small stuff is important. And remember to be nice even when you're fighting. Think before you speak, and avoid saying anything that will leave a lasting scar.

* ***Fake it till you make it.*** Research shows that the more you smile, the happier you actually begin to feel. The same idea can be applied to your relationship. Go out of your way to treat

each other positively, and you may actually start to feel more positively toward one another.

* ***Don't undermine each other.*** You should present a united front to your child. Whenever possible, every decision should be supported by both of you. If Daddy says no TV, then so does Mommy. And vice versa.

* ***Think of each other as comrades.*** Let's face it, you're both fighting in the same parental trench and your survival depends on one another. Treat each other with due respect.

Of course, some conflict is inevitable. But when your kids do see a spat, research suggests that the most important way to prevent the negative outcomes associated with witnessing marital conflict is to make sure they see a *resolution* as well. So even if you and your partner made up behind closed doors, it's a smart idea to reenact the reconciliation in front of your kids.

Unless makeup sex was involved.

Yikes. That would leave some *seriously* lasting scars.

Tips to Help Yourself

Your kid was born with the inherent desire to imitate you. That's kind of the greatest news ever. You do something, he's going to copy it. You do something stupid, and he's *still* going to copy it because he doesn't know any better yet. And this sticking your tongue out thing is really just the beginning. Flared nostril faces, inquisitive eyebrow raises, burps, farts, farts you make with your mouth, farts you make with your armpit, and a whole slew of age-inappropriate words, phrases, and gangsta rap lyrics can be coming out of your offspring's little body before you know it. If you can dream it, and you can demonstrate it, your kid can do it!

Inspiring, isn't it?

One Small Step for Baby

Baby horses are able to walk within an hour of being born. And newborn sharks swim away from their mothers immediately after birth. Thankfully, nature gives us human parents a whole lot more time to prepare for that ~~exhilerating~~ terrifying moment when our children first become independently mobile. But even though your kid won't be able to start walking on her own for a good year or so, you may be surprised to learn that she already has a walking instinct the moment her life begins.

This experiment allows you to *see* your newborn child's walking reflex in action—a lot earlier than you probably ever imagined it was there.

Age	Ability Tested
0–3 months	Motor Skills

What You Need
- ☞ your newborn baby
- ☞ a flat, sturdy surface
- ☞ gravity

How It Works

1. Pick up your tiny, floppy-headed little baby with your hands firmly underneath her arms.

2. Hold her in an upright position, as if she were actually capable of controlling her body well enough to walk, rather than just collapsing into the cute little ball of diaper, skin, and baby fat that she truly is.

3. Position your baby over a flat surface like a table or the floor, with her feet just close enough to touch.

4. Slowly move her forward along the surface, paying close attention to the movements she's making with her legs.

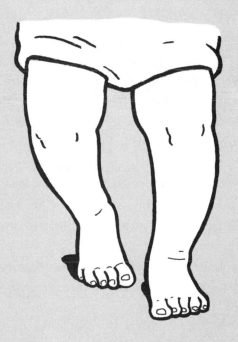

Did you see that? That thing your child was just doing with her feet? She's a newborn, many months away from even thinking about taking her first step, yet she's already making walking movements with her legs! Pretty amazing, huh?

This walking motion is called the "stepping reflex," and it is one of the many reflexive behaviors your baby was born with. In addition to this one, your child was also born with reflexes to suck, to grasp objects in her hands, to splay her toes when the bottom of her foot is stroked, to turn her head and open her mouth toward a touch on her cheek (also known as "rooting"), and to startle at the sound of a loud noise. You know, like when Grandpa nods off with his sweet little grandbaby sleeping snugly in his arms, and then one of them—we're not pointing fingers here—lets one rip so loudly that both of them wake up with a start, looking equally bleary-eyed, confused, and in desperate need of their mommies. Hope you caught that on video—it's bound to go viral.

An interesting thing about the stepping reflex is that although it is already present as soon as your baby is born, it actually *goes away* at about three months old, and it doesn't reemerge until about a year old, when it becomes part of the motion kids use to actually start walking. So what's with the disappearing act? Did your baby suddenly forget how to do this? Did her breast-feeding mommy recently start celebrating happy hour again? The answers are "no" and "maybe, but even if she did, that has nothing to do with this."

The real reason your baby's stepping reflex appears to go away is simply the pull of gravity on her increasingly heavy legs. At about three months your baby's been gaining weight just like she should, but her muscles aren't strong enough yet to pull all that extra mass around. If you perform this experiment at that age, but this time over a moving treadmill or submerged in water—situations that lighten the weight of your baby's legs—you'll be able to see that the stepping reflex hasn't gone away after all. It's still there!

So the next time you're doing a few sets at the gym with your six-month-old or hanging out with her at the pool, take a minute to watch her walk again.

Tips to Help Your Child

Parents buy lots of equipment for their kids in the hope that it will help with their development. One such doodad is the walker. You know, that large boat-like seat on wheels that a child can float around the house on, floundering with her feet and smashing into things while surrounded by giant protective bumpers. The walker is great for a lot of things. It gives you a place to put your baby when you need to finally get a shower. It prevents your baby from emptying all your kitchen cupboards, because try as she might, that walker's giant sides completely block the cupboard doors every time her hands get close enough to reach them. But there's one thing that the walker is *not* great for—teaching your child to walk. In fact, research shows that children who spend the most time in walkers actually experience delays in learning to walk compared to their walker-less friends.

What *will* help your child learn to walk (and to develop a lot of other important motor skills) is to give her some time each day to do what we like to call "baby work." Kids need some time on their own—laying on their mats, playing with their toys, crawling around the house—to practice their motor skills and to explore *sans parents*. Although spending lots of face time talking and playing is important for your child's development, so is letting her do some work on her own. Kids are motivated to explore their surroundings, and by doing so they learn lots of things—even some things we might never even think to try to teach them ourselves. So babyproof the house and watch her go!

Tips to Help Yourself

Even though your kid knows how to take some pseudosteps already, you're going to be doing all the actual walking—and deceptively heavy baby carrying—for quite a while. To give your back a break, we definitely recommend strapping your tyke to your torso with a baby carrier.

Personally, we've found lots of benefits to wearing our babies in a carrier. It keeps the baby happier (in fact, research shows that babies who are worn a couple of hours a day cry less than babies who are not). It lets us get stuff done like housework, shopping, or attending an older child's art class. And it even helps give the little one language-learning opportunities. Having your baby close to your own eye level and in good hearing distance makes it easy to point things out to her in the world—which is great for helping her learn new words!

Scrambled, with Cheeks

Brand-new babies can be pretty hard to read sometimes. Is he smiling at me? Is he smiling at the wall? Or is he smiling because he's about to pee all over this changing table?

This experiment shows you that even though everything your newborn looks at right now is a new and exciting sight for him, he was born with the instinct to find some things more interesting than others.

Age	Ability Tested
0–4 months	Social Development

What You Need

☛ a picture of a normal face next to a picture of a scrambled-up face (which are both conveniently located right here in this book—so don't say we never did anything for you)

How It Works

1. Prop up your wide-eyed little one in a bouncy chair or other safe, comfortable seat.

2. Open this book to the two face pictures in this chapter, and hold them up directly in front of your kid's face.

3. Pay attention to your child's eyes, noting which side of the book—the normal face or the scrambled face—he looks at the longest.

So odds are, your child stared at the normal, unscrambled face longer than the one that was all mixed up. (And if he's anything like our son, he then gave the face a big, beaming smile.)

But why did that happen? The images themselves offer an equal amount of visual interest. They're the same size and color, they contain the exact same shapes, and they're both arranged in a pleasing, symmetric design. The fact that your baby showed a preference for looking at the intact image suggests there is something hardwired into his brain that tells him *the human face is special*.

And it is. After all, humans are social animals, so communicating with other people is a huge deal. And even though it's possible to say quite a bit with a cleverly typed *LOL* or sassy winking emoticon, looking

somebody right in the kisser is still one of the most effective ways for people to connect.

As the person who provides food, blankets, cuddles, and comforting rocks good night at your house, your face in particular is extremely important to your baby—and he knows it. From the time he turned about four days old, your child has been able to distinguish your face from that of a stranger.

This immediate recognition of and preference for faces is especially striking when you consider that infants have really bad eyesight. Although much of a baby's visual anatomy is fully developed inside the womb, he doesn't get to test out any of the equipment until *after* he's born. (After all, it's about as dark as it gets in there!)

As a result, when your baby is born, his vision is so bad that he can only make out objects positioned really close to his face and made up of highly contrasting colors.

So even though you spent a full six months picking out the perfect artichoke-on-asparagus check pattern for your nursery walls (this obviously only applies to your *first* child, since there's no way you'd have the energy for that by the time baby number two comes along), just be aware that your more subtle nursery décor will be lost on your little one at first. If you want to grab his attention with something he'll find truly stimulating to look at, try hanging bold, black-and-white pictures on the crib or over the changing table instead.

Tips to Help Your Child

Although black-and-white pictures will initially be the easiest for your newborn to see, it's important to expose your baby to lots of different visual experiences as well.

Studies have shown that kids who grow up in environments containing a limited variety of lines and shapes for them to stare at all day long end up having a harder time perceiving new angles and shapes later on in life. So although your baby will surely spend lots of time checking out the horizontal and vertical lines that make up your home's walls, doors, and windows, make sure to take him outside to get an eyeful of Mother Nature's twists and turns too.

Reading books and playing patty-cake up close, looking for interesting trees and airplanes at a distance, and even hanging upside down to get a gander at things from a whole new angle can give your child the stimulation he needs to build a strong repertoire of visual skills.

Tips to Help Yourself

The next time Junior seems to have his Pampers in a bunch for no particular reason, and none of the usual fixes like food, sleep, or a freshly diapered butt are getting him to stop crying, try shoving one of those board books filled with photos of baby faces right in front of his.

That cute combination of eyes, noses, and mouths (which you just learned he's been mesmerized by since birth) could be all it takes to give your baby—and you—a much-needed break from the bawling.

Getting a Leg Up

As a parent, you want the best for your kids. You want them to know they can achieve whatever they desire in life, as long as they keep their feet on the ground and keep reaching for the stars.

But as this experiment shows you, all that standing on their feet and reaching with their hands may not necessarily happen *in that order*.

Age	Ability Tested
2–5 months	Motor Skills

What You Need

☞ a toy your baby will be really interested in getting—one of those crazy, crunchy, dangling things that has about 100 different colors and dizzying patterns all over it should be perfect

☞ approximately eight cubic feet of open space (Tough luck, New York City apartment dwellers.)

How It Works

1. Lay your baby on a flat or inclined surface, so he has free movement of both his hands and feet.

2. Hold the toy over your child's legs, just in reaching distance of his feet.

3. Count the number of seconds it takes your child to touch the toy with his feet.

4. Now hold the toy over your child's chest, just in reaching distance of his hands.

5. Count the number of seconds it takes your child to touch the toy with his hands.

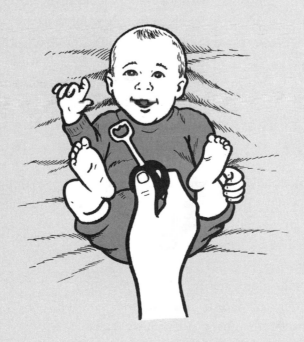

So what did you notice? Is your baby a leg man, or what?

If your kid is like most babies his age, it probably took him less time to reach the toy with his feet than it did with his hands. In fact, he may not have been able to reach the toy with his hands at all yet.

As strange as the idea may seem to opposable-thumb-loving adults like us, young babies can accomplish much more by pointing, reaching, and touching with their feet than they can by trying those same maneuvers with their hands. The reason? It's *easier* for them.

Arms and hands are so useful to us in large part because of the huge range of motion they offer. You can rotate your shoulders, bend your elbows, twist your wrists, and flex your fingers in countless combinations, allowing you to reach just about anywhere and anything you want (except, of course, that one little spot in the middle of your back that really, *really* itches right now).

But it's precisely this amazing flexibility that makes using the upper limbs so tough for babies. Because these parts of their bodies can do so much, it takes a long time for them to master all those movements. In contrast, your lower extremities—unless you're some sort of circus sideshow contortionist—aren't nearly as flexible. Legs move forward and backward, and a little bit from side to side, but that's about it.

So they're a lot simpler to get the hang of right out of the womb.

Tips to Help Your Child

Even though your baby favors his feet right now, his reaching skills are rapidly improving. Pretty soon he's going to be able to reach with his arms like a pro. And when he does, he'll grab anything and everything you leave an arm's length away. Really fast. And with absolutely no warning.

And then he'll probably put it in his mouth.

So if you haven't done so already, now's probably a really good time to start babyproofing that death trap you call a home.

When we were new parents, Andy was going to do some dishes and wanted to put our daughter someplace where she could be close to him.

He got her all set up, and the two of them worked and talked happily. But when Amber walked into the room and saw them, she was horrified. Andy had put Sammy in her little foam baby chair, sitting right on top of the counter directly between a block of knives and an electrical socket.

Seriously. We're not exaggerating.

If you don't know that every bit of that scenario—the chair on the counter, the close proximity to extremely sharp cutting utensils, and the exposed power outlet—is a bad idea, then you need to brush up on your baby safety, just like Andy did.

The point is that hazards are everywhere, and they're easy to miss if you're not thinking about it (or if you're just a typical, learning-on-the-job and completely sleep-deprived new parent). So make sure you take extra care to ensure your baby's environment is safe to explore with his ever-increasing abilities.

The amount of babyproofing you do should be determined by things like how active your baby is, how diligently you plan to watch his every move, the specific hazards in your home, and your personal level of paranoia. Here's a short list of some of the most important things to babyproof, but there's a lot more you could do beyond this. People babyproof other people's houses for a living, for goodness' sake.

* Use plug covers for electrical sockets.

* Confine dangerous substances (cleaners, pesticides, etc.) to a limited number of places and prevent children's access to these places with cupboard latches or another babyproofing method.

* Use baby gates to limit children's access to stairs or other areas unsafe for exploration.

* Educate your baby about dangers to avoid. It might sound silly to explain to your new crawler why she should avoid the stove, but she understands more than you think, and pretty soon that information could prevent a serious injury.

✳ Consult books and online resources on the subject of baby safety and babyproofing.

Tips to Help Yourself

All finished babyproofing your place? Perfect. Now babyproof your face.

Your kid's curious and increasingly powerful fingers *will* at some point end up yanking your earrings, poking your eyes, and lodging themselves right up your nose. So practice your head ducks and defensive eye squints now. Watch some Three Stooges movies for additional ideas about how to escape painful grips applied to sensitive body parts. Then go ahead and enjoy some quality time with your little one.

Baby Boredom

It wasn't all that long ago that a short, scrawny, shrill-voiced version of yourself would annoy your parents to no end with the never-ending complaint, "Mom, Dad, I'm *borrrred*!" Well brace yourself, because karma's heading your way in just a few short years.

But for now—as this experiment will show you—watching your baby get bored is less about giving you a headache and more about giving you a peek inside your child's head.

Age	Ability Tested
2–8 months	Learning

What You Need

☛ two toys that are mildly, but not intensely, interesting for your baby to look at

Good examples: a toy baby bottle, a solid-colored block, or an old-school, "dumb" cell phone you would be embarrassed to be seen with in public

Bad examples: one of those modern touchscreen smartphones babies are riveted by and are somehow born knowing exactly how to use, or a live hamster

How It Works

1. Choose one of the toys and hold it up in front of your baby, making sure to catch her gaze with it. Count how many seconds your baby looks at the toy without breaking eye contact.

2. As soon as she looks away from the toy, immediately catch her eye again with the same toy. Count how many seconds she stares at the object without looking away this time.

3. Keep repeating steps 1 and 2 until you notice your baby starts looking away from the toy after only *two to three seconds*.

4. Drop the first toy you've been using and immediately hold the second toy up for your baby. Count how many seconds she stares at this new toy.

So how'd that turn out? If you ended up with a baby who got really bored of looking at the first toy and then was suddenly interested in playing again when you pulled out the second toy, you just learned something about your child's mind.

Generally, your baby tends to look at things because she finds them interesting. When you initially showed her the first toy, she stared at it for quite a while, taking in all the information she could about it—its shape, its color, whether it appears to be hard or soft, the way the light reflects off of it, approximately how much baby drool it seems to be able to absorb, and so on. As you continually presented the toy to her however, there was less and less *new* information for her to digest, so she looked away sooner and sooner each time. This process of becoming used to, and bored by, an object is called habituation. When your baby's interest in the first toy waned, she is said to have "habituated" to the toy. When you presented the second toy, your baby "dishabituated"—with lots of new information for her to focus her attention on, she suddenly maintained eye contact for a long time again.

The cool thing about habituation is that it can show you what information babies know—or don't know—months before they're old enough to actually talk about it.

For example, if you showed your baby a series of pictures of dogs— one dog after another, after another—eventually she would get habituated to them and stop looking at any new dog picture for longer than a few seconds. So what would happen if you then showed her a picture of a cat? Well, if your baby looked at it for a long time, you could guess she was spending time examining all the new information that creature was presenting her, and thus she knows the difference between dogs and cats. If, however, the cat picture did *not* restore her interest, you could deduce she is not yet able to tell the two species apart. Just like a picture is worth a thousand words, your baby's gaze can tell you way more than a mouthful.

Habituation might even be able to tell you something about your baby's future language skills and IQ, too. Although it seems reasonable to assume that if a child gets bored quickly she'll be doomed to a future filled with ADHD diagnoses and teachers' notes about a "failure to pay attention in class," habituating quickly is actually associated with *positive* outcomes in children. When a child habituates, she has noticed and remembered the important aspects of the object. In other words, she has learned about it. And learning quickly indicates good things for her future.

Unfortunately for all you parents looking for a magic number that tells you how many seconds it should take your baby to habituate for her to be considered a genius, it doesn't exist. It's just that on average, kids who get bored looking at objects more quickly tend to understand more words at a year old and have higher IQs throughout childhood.

Tips to Help Your Child

A basic lesson to draw from this study is that kids get bored with their toys. In the short term, this study shows that you'd better bring more than one toy if you're hoping to entertain your little munchkin through an entire meal at a restaurant. In the long term, this study shows that exposing children to lots of different toys and activities promotes the development of good thinking skills and a healthy brain.

Research on rats provides further evidence that a stimulating environment is important for cognitive development. Rats raised in cages furnished with toys for them to explore became a lot smarter—with larger, more fully developed brains—than their peers raised in toy-free cages. The benefit of the toys was minimized, however, when the rats were continually exposed to the *same* toys.

The same principles hold true for the development of your child's brain. Kids need a stimulating environment full of interesting things to explore. Exposure to the same set of toys and activities over and over limits the information and entertainment a child can glean from her environment. So try to rotate your toys periodically (trading them with other parent friends is an easy way to keep things fresh!), listen to different types of music, engage in various art projects, and discover new places to play.

Tips to Help Yourself

The next time your baby decides that 4:00 AM is the perfect time to wake up (and your better half decides that's the perfect time for *you* to go entertain the kid), let this habituation lesson help you out.

Because you know your bright-eyed little ball of energy is going to get bored with whatever toy you put in front of her before long, gather up *all* the toys your bleary, sleep-encrusted eyes are able to find. Lie down on the floor with your kid in front of you and the pile of toys behind you. Offer her one or two toys to play with, then when you hear her start giving you a "Hey, buddy. I'm habituating over here!" whine, simply grab a new toy and drop it in front of her. With a little practice, and some strategic toy-pile positioning, you can pretty much snooze your way through the entire play session, and your partner never even has to know.

Mad Mobile Skillz

So far in your baby's brief existence on the planet, he hasn't done a whole heck of a lot. He isn't crawling, walking, or chatting with you about your day. He doesn't eat foods that aren't already in liquid or mush form, he hasn't made any pee pees in the potty, and—sorry if this one's a touchy subject for you personally—he might not even be sleeping through the night.

But even though you haven't seen him accomplish any of these big milestones yet, know that he's hard at work *learning* the underlying skills he needs to eventually master them all—and this learning process is happening *all the time*.

This experiment allows you to watch your baby learn a brand-new skill, which should give you insight into how he learns in real life too.

Age	Abilities Tested
3–6 months	Learning, Memory

What You Need

- ☞ a mobile lightweight enough that even a wee little baby could easily move it (Directions for making one are included on pages 38–40 if you don't already have one.)
- ☞ a long piece of ribbon
- ☞ some tape
- ☞ a timer or stopwatch
- ☞ pen and paper

How It Works

☛ **DAY 1**

1. Hang the mobile over the crib, bassinet, or other place where your baby might like to hang out on his back for a while.

2. Tie one end of the ribbon to the mobile, taping over it to make sure it isn't able to slip, and allow the rest of the ribbon to drop straight down to the crib. There should be at least four or five inches of extra ribbon piled up at the bottom.

3. Lay your baby down underneath the mobile so he has a nice, clear view of it.

4. Setting your timer for one minute, count how many times your kid kicks while looking up at the mobile. Write down this number.

5. Gently tie the loose end of the ribbon around one of your baby's ankles. Make sure it's taut enough that the mobile will move whenever he kicks but loose enough that it won't pull at the mobile while his foot is in a resting position.

6. Allow your baby to lay with his foot tied to the mobile for about ten minutes.

7. At the end of the ten minutes, set the timer for one more minute, counting how many times he kicks now. Write down this number.

8. Take the mobile down and save it for tomorrow.

Your kid just learned something. Did you see it?

When you first laid him down, your baby probably checked out the cool mobile overhead and did a little kicking. Nothing out of the ordinary there. But after you tied the mobile to your baby's foot, something changed. He began to notice that each time he kicked, he caused the *mobile* to move!

For a baby who's had no real control of anything that's ever happened to him in his entire life, that's some pretty exciting stuff. You might have even seen the revelation on his face—his eyes may have grown wider, and he may have stared more intently at the mobile. Then he probably started kicking harder, faster, and more frequently.

Even if you didn't notice these changes while they were happening, you should be able to find out right now if they were there. Just compare the two numbers you wrote down during the experiment. Odds are, the second time you counted your kid's kicks, you got a significantly higher number than you did the first time.

Cool, huh?

Your baby learned he could control something. And he liked it. Now let's see how well your child *remembers* what he just learned.

How It Works

☛ DAY 2

1. Hang your mobile in the same place you did yesterday.

2. Lay your baby in the same position as yesterday, but do not tie the ribbon to his ankle.

3. Time your baby for one minute, counting how many times he kicks.

So it's been a whole day since your kid learned his kicks could make this mobile move. And you didn't even tie the mobile to his foot today. But what did you just see?

If the number of kicks you just counted was higher than the *first* number you wrote down yesterday, it shows that not only can your kid learn new things, but he can also *remember* what he has learned over time.

Your baby may seem like he's not doing much these days (other than voicing his displeasure whenever you try to do tummy time), but he's actually capable of learning things and maintaining new information for days. In fact, if you repeat the "Day Two" portion of this experiment once a day over the next several days, he will probably put up high kicking numbers that show how much he remembers each and every time.

One thing that may *not* result in high kick numbers? A change in scenery.

Studies similar to this one have shown that if you change the environment, or *context*, in which a baby learns something, it can negatively affect his ability to remember it. So if you were to repeat "Day Two" again, but this time you hung different objects from the mobile, or covered the bottom and sides of his crib with a brightly colored blanket that wasn't there before, it would likely result in less kicking by your baby.

We often think of learning as a really straightforward process—you study something, and you learn it. But the context in which something is learned really influences our ability to use the new information. And even subtle changes can make a difference.

That's true for adults, too.

Researchers once tested college students' ability to remember what they learned in a particular class. All of the students were taught the material in the same classroom. But when test time came around, half of the students were tested in the room in which they learned, while the other half were tested in a different classroom. It turned out that the context really mattered—the students who were tested in the same place they learned scored much higher.

Tips to Help Your Child

Children appear to be especially sensitive to small changes in context. As you've seen in this experiment, babies will have difficulty remembering what they learned if the mobile or the crib looks different. Other research has shown that preschool children who are taught an object's name while the object is sitting on a tablecloth with one pattern (like blue with pictures of fish) will have trouble remembering the object's name when it's sitting on a tablecloth with a different pattern (like red with yellow squares). Which is crazy, because the tablecloth it's laying on seems to have nothing at all to do with learning what something is called.

You can help your child overcome his difficulty remembering things in different contexts by teaching him about the same thing in multiple environments. Those preschool children who had trouble remembering an object's name when tested on a new tablecloth showed substantial improvement if they learned about the object while it was sitting on several different tablecloths instead of always learning about it while it sat on the same one.

What this means for you is that teaching your child about something in multiple locations can help him to be less reliant on the context to remember. For example, rather than only talking about it at dinnertime in your kitchen, introduce the word "fork" to him in other places too, like when you see them in restaurants, at the store, in books, or if you happen to find yourself with your entire family on a farm baling hay for some reason. It'll help him pick up the word more quickly. (Plus he might help you pick up some of that hay.)

Try to keep the effect of context in mind as you interact with your child over the years. Giving him word problems to figure out as you're waiting for your dinner to be served at a restaurant or standing in line at the supermarket instead of only talking about math at your normal homework time and location may eventually boost his SAT scores!

Tips to Help Yourself

Your baby's ability to learn and remember information over time explains why most babies know their names by the time they are about five months old. And at about six or seven months old, they've already figured out that the word "Mommy" or "Daddy" refers to you.

Don't want to wait that long?

Well, if you're the type of parent who's really itching to hear that first "Mama" or "Dada" come out of your kid's lips as soon as humanly possible—or if you really want to make sure your kid says your name before your partner's—don't just stick your big crazy face two inches away from your baby's and belt out, "Say Mama! Say Mama!" all the time like a sucker.

Give him the lesson in a variety of contexts!

"Yes, Baby, *Mama* is feeding you." "Hi, Cutie! *Mama* is waving at you from all the way across the room!" "What's that taped on every single page of your favorite picture book, Sweetie? Why it's just a bunch of glossy eight-by-ten photos of *Mama*!" "Sure you can play with my phone, Honey! Just watch this video of *Mama* saying *Mama* on an endlessly repeating loop!"

Pull a few stunts like these, and *Dada* doesn't stand a chance.

Making a Simple Mobile

If you're a supercrafty Martha Stewart type, your mobile is going to look *good*. We can see it now: a tastefully chosen color palette, ribbon bows you'd expect to pay six dollars apiece for at an upscale greeting card boutique, delicately balanced crossbeams from which twirl whimsical illustrations of emus and hippopotamuses frolicking among the rhododendrons . . .

For the rest of you, your mobile is going to look weird. Trust us, we made one.

Despite all the time you spend trying to balance the pencils so they hang straight, they won't. No matter how gingerly you apply the tape, it'll still end up bumpy. Your mobile will never grace the cover of *Beautiful Parent Craft Projects* magazine. But the good news is, it doesn't have to. As long as the mobile you make is attention grabbing and your infant can move it, it should work perfectly for this experiment!

Your completed mobile should look something like this:

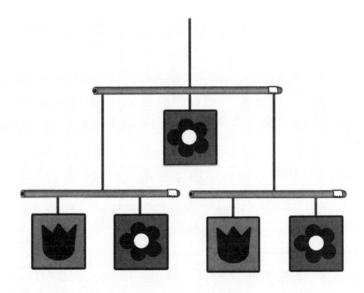

Materials

☛ 3 *unsharpened* pencils (Let's avoid sharp objects, just in case the mobile falls down.)

☛ ribbon

☛ tape

☛ card stock

☛ hole punch

☛ scissors

Instructions

1. Tie three ribbons to one of the pencils: a longer one secured to the middle and shorter ones secured to each end. The middle ribbon will support the mobile while it hangs, and the other two ribbons will support additional pencils.

2. Tie the ribbons you have secured at the ends of the first pencil to the middles of two other pencils. Try to tie each ribbon so the pencils are as balanced as possible when hanging.

3. Create five cardstock cutouts to hang from the mobile. We made simple black squares that our older daughter decorated with stickers. The specific shape and design of your cutouts doesn't matter as long as the mobile is visually interesting.

4. Use the hole punch to make holes in your cardstock cutouts that will be used to suspend them with ribbon.

5. Attach your cardstock cutouts to the mobile with short ribbons. Secure one to the middle of the top pencil, and secure one to each end of the other two pencils.

6. Place tape over all of the places where you have tied ribbons. After all, you want them to stay in place when your baby starts kicking this thing like crazy!

Tipsy Tots

Who's more fun to hang out with: babies or drunk people? Tough decision, isn't it?

Well thanks to this experiment, you no longer have to choose. By combining the undeniable cuteness of your child with the delightfully unsteady dizziness of somebody who's *always down to party,* this could very well be the most fun you've ever had learning about science.

And oh yeah. It's actually good for your kid, too.

Age	Ability Tested
3–12 months	Motor Skills

What You Need
- ☞ your baby
- ☞ an office chair or other chair that can spin completely around in a circle, over and over and over
- ☞ a barf bag (if spinning completely around in a circle, over and over and over isn't exactly your thing)

How It Works

1. Take a seat in your favorite spinning chair, holding your baby on your lap facing forward.

2. Quickly spin the chair to the left, making sure to abruptly stop when you return to your starting position.

3. Wait 30 seconds, then spin to the left (and abruptly stop) again.

4. Repeat steps 2 and 3, only this time, spin your chair to the right.

5. Keep the good times going by repeating steps 2 through 4 with your baby lying on her left side, and then again while she's lying on her right side.

So did your baby love this experiment, or what?

If she's like most kids her age, she was totally into it. Babies *love* to be jostled around—whether it's by spinning, rocking, bouncing, swinging, or even tossing. This is because babies are born with a highly developed *vestibular system*, the collection of canals and organs inside your inner ear that senses the body's movement and degree of balance. Messing with your vestibular system—either by spinning in a chair as an infant, or by siphoning Natty Light through a three-story-tall beer bong in college—can produce disorienting and dizzying sensations.

In other words, it's a whole lot of fun.

But doing this experiment with your kid is about more than just pure entertainment. Researchers have found that intentionally stimulating your baby's vestibular system in this way offers real benefits to the development of your child's reflexes and motor skills. In one study, babies who were spun four times a week for four weeks met motor development milestones like sitting, crawling, standing, and walking more quickly than their peers who did not undergo the chair-spin treatment.

So if you're an aggressive alpha parent who's already decided that your brand-new baby *will* be receiving multiple full-ride basketball scholarship offers eighteen years from now, here's an easy way to give the kid a head start.

But even if you don't have such specific and lofty goals for your offspring, you can still repeat this experiment on multiple occasions to observe its effect on your baby over time. Start your spin sessions anytime when your baby is between the ages of three and twelve months old—but remember that the earlier you start, the more potential benefit for your child. For maximum results, try repeating the procedure with your baby four times each week over the next four weeks, for a total of sixteen sessions.

Tips to Help Your Child

Here's something else vestibular stimulation is good for: calming your baby.

Think about it. When your little angel is crying her precious little head off, what's the quickest way to get her quiet and contented? You pick her up, pat her on the back, and bounce her around the room, of course!

This strategy works so well because bouncing or rocking is a form of vestibular stimulation, and studies have shown that babies find vestibular stimulation extremely soothing—more soothing, in fact, than merely touching her or talking to her in a reassuring voice. By the time they get to be six to eight months old, many babies even start calming *themselves* by rocking, bouncing, swaying, or head-banging. So it turns out your kid is not screaming until you drop everything and go pick her up *just* to torture you (although it sometimes feels that way). She's really just asking you to give her the calming little jostle she needs.

Tips to Help Yourself

Although your kid could happily spin around in your chair all day, *you'll* probably want to take a break before too long. That's because the vestibular system begins to decline with age—so people tend to get wussier and wussier about motion sickness as they get older.

But the good news is, you're not that old yet. So have as much fun as you can with this experiment now, because you're probably not going to want to repeat it later on with the grandkids.

Now You See It . . .

Having kids is awesome for tons of reasons, not the least of which is how freaking cool you seem to your little one.

In your child's eyes, you're super tall, totally strong, and you know the answer to any question imaginable.

Do this experiment, and you can add "mind-blowing magician extraordinaire" to your already impressive parental résumé.

Age	Ability Tested
7–9 months	Problem Solving

What You Need

- ☞ a flat surface
- ☞ a burp cloth
- ☞ a toy small enough that you can easily place it on that flat surface and cover it with the burp cloth
- ☞ no actual magic skills whatsoever

How It Works

1. Lay the burp cloth out flat right in front of your child, so it's easily within his reach.

2. Show your child the toy and get him interested in it. You can even let him hold it for a second or two, if that helps capture his attention.

3. Remind yourself that you are *not actually a magician*, nor are you trying to be one right now.

4. While your kid is watching you, and *without trying to hide what you're doing one bit*, take the toy and place it under the burp cloth. There should be a big, obvious lump in the cloth where the toy is hidden.

5. See what your kid does.

So there are a couple of ways this experiment might have gone for you.

If your kid was completely baffled by this "disappearing act" and he didn't even try looking under the burp cloth to see where the toy went, congratulations! You apparently are the Houdini of your household.

Actually, there's a much more plausible explanation for why this admittedly unsophisticated trick works with younger children—they haven't yet achieved *object permanence*. Object permanence is just a fancy-pants psychology way of saying that you know objects are stable and permanent and keep on existing *even if you can't see them.*

Kids don't normally get that concept until they're about eight months old. But once they do, this trick won't work on them at all. After your kid figures out that things don't fall off the face of the earth every time they're out of his view, he'll be able to easily find the toy you've been hiding under the burp cloth—and he'll also be able to search for a ball the next time it rolls under the couch.

Recent research has led child development experts to believe that your kid may actually understand object permanence (at least a little bit) well before he is able to show it in this experiment. In one study, six-month-olds retrieved the hidden toy when they were allowed to reach for it immediately, but not when they were made to wait. Another ingeniously designed study involved showing three-month-olds a rabbit toy moving back and forth across a stage, then moving behind a screen with a window in it. When the rabbit passed behind the window, it seemed to disappear—and the babies were surprised, indicating they knew the rabbit should not have disappeared.

(By the way, we would have included that experiment in this book, but it involves constructing a complex apparatus and the ability to keep your infant still for quite a while to watch it. Good luck with that, considering you're still trying to master the trick of changing his diaper without letting him squirm off the changing table.)

Tips to Help Your Child

Your kid is naturally curious and motivated to explore his surroundings. He is always taking in his environment and using it to learn important lessons about the world, including object permanence. That's why it's important that you think about the type of environment you create for your baby.

When considering how the sights and sounds around him may influence his ability to learn, deciding whether and when to expose your child to television is a really big deal.

We're not the kind of parents that say TV is all bad all the time. In fact, movie night is a cherished tradition in our family. But TV *is* something parents should be very careful with.

And here's why:

TV can interfere with children's learning in a couple of ways. First, it can prevent kids from doing the kind of experiential play that is really important for their cognitive development. Just like your mind tends to turn off in front of the TV, so does your kid's. (You can tell this by the characteristic gaping mouth and zombie eyes that befall any kid plunked in front of a big screen.) You may think that the TV's just on in the background, but it's extremely captivating for your child. He ends up zoning out in front of it, and pretty soon none of that really important brain-building exploration is going on.

But the biggest danger of TV is that it can interfere with your child's interaction with *you*. And because interaction with you is probably the most crucial way to promote your child's language and cognitive development, this can be extremely bad for your child. Kids learn more from simply talking to you than they could ever learn from watching TV. Study after study has compared a child's ability to learn something from a live person versus a TV—and the live person always wins. There is something special about one-on-one interaction that cannot be captured by TV. (Yes, even "educational TV" is no substitute for *you*.)

So the next time you go to turn on the TV, think twice. Consider whether you could possibly spend the same time talking, playing, or reading instead of zoning out.

Tips to Help Yourself

Just as your baby is learning that objects are stable and permanent, he's learning the same thing about you, too. So now when you leave the house to go to work, or just leave the room to go pour yourself a well-deserved

"Mommy and Daddy drink," he knows that you still exist, you must be somewhere else, and he wants you to come back—right now!

So don't be surprised if his advancing cognitive development is accompanied by increasingly difficult good-byes. Hopefully this separation anxiety won't prove as traumatic for you as it is for your kid.

But if it does, maybe a *second* "Mommy and Daddy drink" is in order.

. . . Now You Don't

J ust because your kid is learning new and amazing things every day, it doesn't mean she has everything figured out just yet.

This experiment exposes some limitations of your smarty-pants's newfound object permanence—which is exactly the kind of information you need to help you get your phone, keys, wallet, or anything else you prefer to keep slobber-free out of your young mess maker's hands.

Age	Ability Tested
8–10 months	Problem Solving

What You Need

- ☞ a flat surface
- ☞ 2 identical burp cloths
- ☞ 1 toy small enough that you can easily cover it with either of those burp cloths
- ☞ a kid who is no longer fooled by the "magic trick" you pulled in Experiment #9

How It Works

1. Lay the two burp cloths out flat right in front of your child so they're a couple inches apart from each other and both are easily within your child's reach.

2. Show your child the toy and get her interested in it. You can even let her hold it for a second or two, if that helps capture her attention.

3. While your kid is watching you, and *without trying to hide what you're doing one bit*, take the toy and place it under one of the burp cloths.

4. Ask your kid to get the toy. After she retrieves it, tell her "Great job!" and take the toy from her.

5. Immediately repeat steps 3 and 4 three more times or until your child has successfully retrieved the toy under the same burp cloth four times in a row.

6. Making sure your child is still watching, immediately hide the toy under the *other* burp cloth.

7. Ask her to get the toy.

8. See what she does this time.

This experiment illustrates a classic error made by children at this age. Hide a toy and they can find it. But hide a toy multiple times in one location, then hide it in a second location, and suddenly they don't know what to do.

Even though your baby now has object permanence (the knowledge that objects don't disappear just because they're out of view), she suddenly can't find the toy. Why would this be? Why is it that she can find the toy when you hide it in one location over and over, but can't find it when the hiding location is changed? She can even see the bulge the toy makes under the burp cloth! What the heck is wrong with this kid?

Multiple explanations have been put forth for why children commit this error. One explanation is that when children initially learn object permanence, it's not perfect. Your child doesn't go from believing objects magically disappear when she can't see them to suddenly knowing objects have enduring properties that persist even when out of sight. Development isn't as fast and smooth as the flip of a light switch. Instead, kids *kind of* understand and *sometimes* understand before they *fully* understand all the time.

A second explanation for why children commit this error is that continually reaching to the same location creates a motor rhythm that is hard to break. So far your child has reached left, left, left, left. . . . Suddenly you want her to go right, and she has a hard time breaking her keep-reaching-to-the-left momentum to do it. And there's some good evidence for this explanation: if you reposition your child before hiding the toy under the second burp cloth (you could move her from sitting on your lap to standing on your lap, for example), there's a good chance it will help break the rhythm that reaching to one location has built up, enabling her to find the toy in the second location.

It's a cool trick. But alas, it's a short-lived one. In a couple of months, none of these confusing aspects of the task will pose a problem for your kid anymore. She'll know without a doubt that objects exist even when they're out of sight, and tricks like switching your hiding spot will no longer fool her.

Tips to Help Your Child

Even though your kid now understands object permanence, this experiment just proved that if the circumstances are right, she might not always be able to show you what she knows. Here's another example of that. Research shows that kids may understand 150 words or more before they can say a single one. That's why toddlers can often follow simple instructions—like "Get the ball"—before they can *say* the related words—like "ball."

The lesson to be learned here? Don't sell your child short. (Also, it's easy to get kids to fetch things like balls.)

Parents often fail to realize how many words their children understand. So they also fail to take opportunities to expand their child's knowledge, figuring that the kid won't understand what they're saying anyway. But your child usually understands more than you think. And even if she doesn't understand yet, she soon will. Talking to her as much as possible will help her along.

Here are some simple tips for increasing the amount that you talk to your child:

* *Think of your child as a conversation partner no matter what her language level.* Even a child who does not say any words yet is responsive in nonverbal ways. And the more you talk with her, the quicker she will take up her side of the conversation.

* *Don't be afraid to use big words.* Often parents mistakenly think that they should always keep things as simple and repetitive as possible. In actuality, the broader a vocabulary you use with your child, the broader her vocabulary will be.

* *Narrate and explain.* Add words to your day by narrating what you're doing and explaining things to your child. Talk about the steps you're taking to bake cookies. Describe the difference between a moth and that butterfly over there. Outline your position on whatever shocking celebrity breakup you're currently obsessing about. Just keep talking—because you never know what she'll pick up.

Tips to Help Yourself

Because it's true that you never know what your kid will pick up (but you can safely bet that she *will* pick up all of the most valuable and easily breakable stuff you own if you leave her alone with it for two seconds), it's a good idea to put the lessons learned from this experiment to work for you.

For example, if your baby can't seem to keep her grubby little hands off your phone during dinner, no problem. Just hide it under your napkin right there on the table. Sure, your child will be able to lift up that napkin and find the phone a few times in a row, but then BLAMMO! As soon as you hide it under a *second* napkin, the kid will suddenly be as clueless as the day she was born.

Bonus Tip: While your child is staring in dumbfounded, openmouthed amazement at your disappearing phone trick, take full advantage of the situation by shoving some spinach or other leafy green vegetable down her hatch. You've probably only got seconds before she snaps out of her stupor, so act fast!

My Kind of Doll

Are you concerned about the friends your baby is hanging out with? Is he crawling with a fast crowd? Teething with a bunch of troublemakers? Doing tummy time on the wrong side of the tracks?

Of course not. He's a baby. So you choose all of his friends for him.

But someday soon, your little angel will start deciding what kind of people he wants to spend time with *all by himself*. And as this experiment will show you, he already has the tools that will help him make those decisions *right now*.

Age	Ability Tested
10–12 months	Social Development

What You Need

- ☛ 2 different snacks your baby likes
- ☛ 2 bowls to put those snacks in
- ☛ 2 similar-looking (but not completely identical) dolls, puppets, or stuffed animals—a lion and a tiger would work, as would two teddy bears wearing different colored overalls (We bet you already have these, because for some reason far beyond our comprehension, the companies that make teddy bears just love to put them all in overalls. . . . Are we right or are we right?)

How It Works

1. Offer the two bowls of food to your child and tell him to pick *one* of the snacks to eat. Note which one he goes for, then take the two bowls and place them in front of the dolls.

2. Put on a little puppet show for your kid! First, have one of the puppets stick its face into the first food bowl, make a bunch of sloppy eating noises, and then say, "Ewww, yuck. I *don't* like that!" Then have the same puppet make eating noises over the second food bowl and say, "Mmmm, yum. I *like* that!"

3. Perform the exact same scene with the other puppet, except have this puppet like and dislike the *opposite* foods the first one did. (For example, if the first doll liked cereal and disliked blueberries, the second doll should like blueberries and dislike cereal.)

4. Hold both dolls side by side in front of your child, and ask him to pick one to play with. See which one your kid touches first.

Did you notice anything about the playdate your little one just scheduled?

The doll your child wanted to play with at the end of the experiment was probably the one that liked the same snack your child chose at the beginning of the experiment. Seems like a rather trivial way to pick a new BFF, we know, but you just watched your kid do it.

What this shows you is that your baby—who isn't even old enough to talk yet—is already observing others and making judgments about them. And what *are* these judgments exactly? He apparently favors puppets (and people) who are similar to him.

The similarities and differences that drive these preferences don't even have to be big ones to produce the same results. If you used dramatically different snacks in this experiment, like offering a choice between brussels sprouts and a brownie, you could rationalize that kids preferred the stuffed animals who chose like them because they simply *exhibited good taste*. But because you used two snacks you know your kid likes, the decision became totally arbitrary. In fact, you could have offered a choice as tiny as that between one kind of cracker and another, and your child still would've been biased toward the doll that preferred the same cracker he did.

Want to do the experiment without having to dust-bust a bunch of crumbs afterward? It works with nonfood preferences too! Researchers conducting this experiment have found that infants will favor a puppet who wears the same colored gloves as them over a puppet wearing different colored gloves.

The craziest thing is, what you're seeing displayed in your young child right now is *not* isolated to this particular time in his life. It's really a sign of things to come.

Research has documented that people of all ages, whether they're babies, tweens, new parents, or great-grandparents, tend to show a preference toward others who are like them in some way. These preferences can be based off arbitrary similarities like the food choice in this study, or more meaningful ones like gender, cultural background, or a shared love of ironic, old-timey facial hairstyles.

Being attracted to people similar to yourself can benefit your romantic relationships as well. Contrary to the old saying "opposites attract," research shows that when people are looking for someone worth changing their relationship status for, they tend to be more attracted to others who are similar to them in ways like intelligence, education level, family background, religious affiliation, and even height. And some evidence suggests that marriages whose partners share more similarities may even be happier and longer lasting.

Tips to Help Your Child

It's totally natural for your youngster to develop biases toward others based on the similarities and differences he perceives. The upside of this tendency is that it helps him make sense of the world and where he fits into it. But the downside, as you can imagine, is the possibility it could lead to harmful stereotypes and prejudices that won't do anybody any good.

Having conversations with your child about people's similarities and differences can increase the understanding he shows toward others and decrease any negative attitudes that might try creeping into his psyche. If you already feel comfortable chatting about that kind of thing with your kid, that's great! But having such overt conversations about discrimination and the like isn't all that common. In fact, many parents take the approach of *avoiding* talking about these things with their children altogether, hoping this will somehow make them treat all people equally, becoming blind to their "meaningless" differences.

The problem is, this study just showed you that your kid is already affected by some of the most meaningless differences you could think of—so talking about it is still your best bet.

Tips to Help Yourself

Don't really feel like *talking* to your kid about heavy subjects like prejudice? You could try exposing him to books or age-appropriate videos that tackle those topics instead. But you might want to preview your selections first. Even though children's stories almost always end positively, with all of the characters being nice and getting along swimmingly, they often start out with conflict based on characters exhibiting nasty, negative behaviors.

Polly Pig skips school to go roll around in the mud all day. Buddy Bear steals honey from his grandma's beehive. And Charles Woodchuck bullies his little brother by giving him a swirly. If your kid isn't already partaking in these kinds of behaviors, seeing them in a book or show might give him new ideas for being bad that he hadn't ever thought of on his own.

You've got your hands full enough as it is. Don't inadvertently help your kid team up with a bad influence—even a fictional one.

The Second Year

Congratulations on making it through your child's first year! If you could do *that*, then the rest of your job as a parent is going to be a total cakewalk. That's a complete lie, of course. Everything is going to get exponentially harder from here.

But you *have* done an awesome job in these first twelve months. So let's sit back for a second to marvel at all of the impressive developing your child has done so far—and the huge role you played in helping her do so.

OK, that's enough.

You'd better stop celebrating and go find your one-year-old, because the chances are really, really high that she has just gotten into and made a huge mess of something you didn't even remember you owned. And while you're up, plan to stay there, because your kid is going to grow and change so fast this year that it will often be tough to keep up with her.

This is going to be another year of tremendous growth for your child. But unlike last year, when she started out with limited skills and was easily contained, she's beginning this year as an already mobile, muttering, and manipulative little run for your money. And by the end of this year, she will seem as different to you as her current self does from the tiny newborn you first met.

Over the next year your child will pick up lots of words, begin using tools like hairbrushes, toothbrushes, and paintbrushes (and sometimes *not* mix up which one is used where!), learn to recognize herself as the unique person she is, and start to understand that other people have different thoughts and perceptions than she does. This growth will be so fast and break so many new boundaries that it might look like a whirlwind of overwhelming activity.

Lucky for you, these experiments are here to help you put everything on pause—and make some sense of it all.

The Honeydew Whisperer

Ever catch yourself reciting the contents of your shopping list out loud while you're walking through the grocery store? Or reenacting—and improving upon—some awkward story you told at last week's neighborhood block party?

It's a little embarrassing, right?

Your kid, on the other hand, is way too young to feel weird about carrying on a conversation all by herself. Which is great news for you, since it means you'll be able to do this pretty hilarious experiment. (And learn just how socially adept your kid already is, too.)

Age	Abilities Tested
12–14 months	Language Development, Social Development

What You Need

- ☞ an inanimate object that has no face (like a melon, a fuzzy slipper, or even a ball of dryer lint)
- ☞ a hiding place large enough to conceal you or another adult
- ☞ the ability to stifle laughter while making your kid look silly
- ☞ a grown-up partner in crime

How It Works

1. Have one adult hide in a room completely out of sight, while stealthily holding up the inanimate object in full view. For example, you could crouch behind a table and hold the object so it appears to be sitting on top of the table.

2. Have a second adult bring your baby into the room and put her in a high chair or some other kid-containing seat directly across from the object. Your child and the faceless object should be "facing" each other. (We know that doesn't make any sense, but it kind of does. Trust us.)

3. Making sure your kid is paying attention, the visible adult should engage in a "conversation" with the inanimate object for about one minute. After each thing the adult says, the hidden person should make the object "respond"—making whirring or beeping sounds for the object's voice, while also wagging the object around a little bit as it "talks." The conversation should go something like this:

    ADULT: Hi. How are you?
    OBJECT: (*Turns to "face" the speaker before responding.*) Mrr, mrrr, mrrr, mrr.
    ADULT: I'm fine, thanks.
    OBJECT: Mrr, mrrr, mrrr, mrr.
    ADULT: Really? That's interesting.
    OBJECT: Mrr, mrrr, mrrr, mrr.
    ADULT: OK. Bye.
    OBJECT: Mrr, mrrr, mrrr, mrr.
    ADULT: (*Waves goodbye to the object and exits the room.*)

4. The hidden person should then make the object turn back so it's "facing" your child again and wait for her to either vocalize (make any vocal sound) or move.

5. Each time your child does one of these things, the hidden person should treat it as a conversational turn, making the object respond to your kid in the same way it did during the conversation with the adult.

6. See how long you can keep this ridiculousness going.

You sneaky trickster. You just duped your innocent little sweetie pie into making friends with a melon. And it was surprisingly easy, wasn't it?

The way you manipulated this completely lifeless object—turning it to "face" a speaker and having it respond whenever it was spoken to—made it seem very lifelike. And even though your child is only a year old, she's sophisticated enough to pick up on these social cues and treat the object accordingly.

The fact that your kid so readily shot the breeze with something whose appearance in no way resembled a person's shows you just how social she is by nature. She wants to talk. She needs to communicate. And as a parent whose head is not made of fruit, you're her perfect conversation partner. Here's why:

* **You're motivated.** Who cares more than you about your child's language development? No one. That's why you're willing to give her lots of practice.

* **You ask questions.** Parents tend to ask more questions, which gives kids more practice talking.

* **You have shared knowledge with your child.** Because you share lots of experiences with your child, you have lots to talk about. You know which cartoon pony she's most likely to gush about this week, just like you know which animal at the zoo she'll say smells the most like poop. (Surprisingly, it's the flamingos.) This helps make your conversations richer and longer.

* **It's easier than you might think.** All you have to do is open your mouth. Talk to her about everything—how cute she is, which sounds go with which barnyard animals, how much laundry you have to do, the current gubernatorial election, whatever. The content isn't as important as the effort. So just make sure you make one!

We know that right now your child probably doesn't have much of a vocabulary, so most of her responses to you will not be in words. But don't let that fool you into thinking she's not being communicative. She totally is, in whatever ways she can. So always acknowledge whatever response she does give you—be it a word, grunt, look, gesture, or burp—and treat it as her conversational turn. Pretty soon her unintelligible responses will turn into full-fledged sentences, and you'll no longer be carrying the full weight of your conversations.

And it will happen so gradually that you won't even be able to tell when it did!

Tips to Help Your Child

Responding to your child's attempts at communication is one of the best ways to promote language development, and you can start doing it as soon as your baby is born!

When you hear your little one use her little voice (whether she's saying a complete word or just a single vowel or consonant), be sure to acknowledge her by talking about what she's doing, smiling and nodding, or even giving her a simple, well-timed touch. These in-the-moment responses are rewarding to your child and encourage her to keep communicating.

When our daughter was little, we made sure to frequently acknowledge her in these ways when she made attempts to speak. Sometimes we even found ourselves overtly telling her, "We love your little voice. We love it when you talk." Probably not coincidentally, she ended up being an early talker and developing a large vocabulary early on—which are both common outcomes for children of parents who are more responsive to their children's attempts to communicate. And we only regret it a little bit now when we ask her to please stop yell-singing at the top of her lungs and she retorts, "You're joking. I know you love my voice!"

Tips to Help Yourself

When you do want your talkative kid to hush for just a few minutes so you can check your voicemail, put the new baby down for a nap, or try to figure out where the missing cat's meow is coming from, there are a couple things to try.

First, you can always resort to the tried-and-true "quiet game" your own parents probably used on you a time or two. It's the one that goes something like this: "Hey, kiddo. Let's see who can be quiet the longest! Go!" When your kid "wins," you really win.

Another option is to remember that although it's great to talk with your kid, you don't have to do it constantly. Give her some time on her own to explore and interact with her environment. This experiment shows that she'll be able to blabber on with just about anything she finds around the house, after all! Plus this kind of independent play can benefit her cognitive and motor development—and give you a break, too!

Do I Know You?

By now, your baby knows you pretty darn well. He knows your face, your voice, and even your smell. He knows you'll stick food in his face when he's hungry, and read to him when he puts a book in front of yours.

So what happens when he looks up and realizes the pant leg he's tugging on doesn't belong to you? Does he take it in stride, or try to run and hide?

This classic child development experiment will give you some insight into just how attached to you your former fetus still is—by having you swap places with a complete stranger.

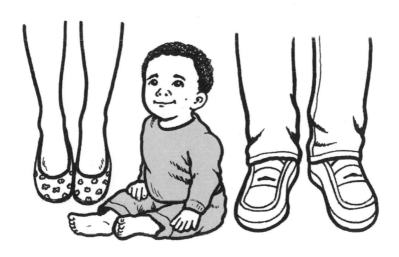

Age	Ability Tested
12–18 months	Social Development

What You Need

☞ you

☞ your child

☞ a room containing two chairs and some toys on the floor

☞ someone who is a stranger to your child (but not to you since that would be kind of sketchy)

How It Works

1. Enter the room with your child, take a seat in one of the chairs, and allow your child to explore the toys on the floor. Do this for about three minutes.

2. Have the stranger enter the room, greet you, and quietly sit down in the other chair. Wait three minutes again.

3. While the stranger distracts your child, leave the room. After you're gone, the stranger should stay in the room and play with your child for another three minutes.

4. Return to the room and let the stranger leave. Stay in the room with your child for—you guessed it—three minutes.

5. Leave the room without the stranger returning this time, so your child stays in the room by himself for three minutes.

6. Have the stranger return to be with your child for three minutes.

7. Come back into the room, and have the stranger leave, one last time.

Feeling like you (or your child) could use some wine (or whole milk) about now? We get it. That may have been a pretty stressful situation for both of you. If the mere thought of doing this experiment traumatizes you too much to even try it, don't worry. You can still get some idea of how your baby might do in this test by paying attention to how he reacts when you leave and return in real-life situations, like when he stays with a new babysitter or unfamiliar relative.

All of the crazy parent-stranger shuffling this experiment had you do—just you in the room, both you and the stranger in the room, just the stranger in the room, and no adult in the room—was designed to examine the attachment level that exists between you and your child. There are many ways your kid could have reacted to this situation, ranging from completely freaking out whenever you slipped out of sight to nonchalantly accepting this strange adult he's never met before as his permanent new caretaker. (Sorry if that second option happened to you. That's really got to sting.)

The reaction you should be shooting for—which psychologists refer to as *secure attachment*—falls right in the middle of those two extremes. A child is considered securely attached if he strikes a healthy balance between wanting to be near you, while also wanting to independently explore his environment. In this experiment, that would've looked something like this:

* Whenever you were around, your kid actively explored the room, checking out the toys, walking all around, and playing freely and comfortably.

* When you were absent, your kid explored and played less.

* Whenever you returned to the room after being gone, your kid was happy to see you and made efforts to be close to you again.

A securely attached child would be curious about and receptive to the stranger but would *not* see the stranger as a substitute for you (as evidenced by his happiness when you returned). Likewise, if you felt weird about leaving, didn't like seeing him get upset when you were gone, and wanted to scoop him up and make it all better every time you got back, chances are the two of you are securely attached.

Secure attachment bodes well for both of you. It means your child considers you a comforting, reliable presence he can count on. He feels safe exploring his environment, because he knows you will always be there for him. It also means your child probably cries less during everyday separations, responds positively to your returns, and is pretty responsive to you and your commands (even if it doesn't always seem like it). It also predicts good things for his future. Infants who are securely attached tend to exhibit better psychological well-being and physical health, have more successful romantic relationships, and engage in less substance abuse through adulthood.

So what if your child did *not* display textbook secure attachment behavior during this experiment? What if he continued exploring the toys whether you were there or not, got intensely anxious or upset, or avoided you upon your return? Don't be too worried about any of it, because a child's attachment behavior can vary quite a bit. Kids who show secure attachment behavior at a year old may not do so at a year and a half—or vice versa. And after that eighteen-month mark, you won't even be able to do this test anymore, since situations involving strangers naturally become less stressful, and children become better able to cope with distance from a parent.

Traditionally, attachment has been assessed in terms of a child's relationship to his mother. But the attachment relationship is not confined to the mother role. Children can also become securely attached to other people who play important roles in their lives, including fathers, siblings, peers, grandparents, day-care providers, and anyone else who is a frequent, loving presence.

We learned firsthand how strong *sibling* attachment can be after we started leaving our second child with a babysitter and found that he was never fazed by it one bit! At first we took it personally, guessing that he just wasn't as attached to us as his sister had been at the same age. But then we took him on his first outing *without* his sister, and we saw a whole different baby. Rather than leaving us to explore freely, he clung to us and wouldn't even play unless we were right there next to him. That's when it hit us—he had always been so comfortable, even in new circumstances with strangers, because he was securely attached to his sister.

Tips to Help Your Child

One of the best ways to establish a secure attachment with your child is to be sensitive and responsive to his needs. Researchers have found that parents with securely attached children tend to read their children's signals well and to respond to them quickly. Picking your child up when he wants closeness, or soothing him if he cries, communicates to him that you are attentive, available, and reliable.

But being responsive and sensitive doesn't mean overly coddling your child and preventing him from ever feeling *any* discomfort. In fact, your child needs to struggle at times in order to learn important skills.

For example, allowing your child to learn how to soothe himself to sleep (instead of rushing in with open arms and exposed breasts every time you hear him whimper) can help him *and you* sleep a whole lot better. And letting him work out problems by himself can help him build all sorts of other valuable skills too. So don't immediately put those puzzle pieces together when you see him fumbling with them for a second, and don't blurt out the correct answer to a math problem until he's had time to try working through the thing himself. Kids who are allowed to struggle a little bit through challenges ultimately learn that by putting in more effort—even when it's hard—they can reach a satisfying solution on their own.

If you've been practicing the behaviors recommended here and still haven't managed to build the ideal attachment, don't beat yourself up. You are only half of this relationship, after all. Aspects of your child's personality, like how socially oriented, difficult, or easygoing he is, can affect the relationship you're building. Be sure to keep giving him lots of love and warmth, tempered with guidance and limitations, and you will be doing the best thing you can do to promote positive emotional development.

Tips to Help Yourself

If you've ever left your kids with a babysitter so you could head out for a well-deserved (and probably long overdue) date night, you may have experienced some of this "stranger experiment" in real life. Here are some tips for making these potentially traumatic sitter swaps easier:

* When you have a new babysitter, spend some time hanging out all together before you leave your child alone with her. Invite the sitter over for a short visit on a day you will be home with your kid and spend about an hour just playing on the floor. Encourage the babysitter and your kiddo to play together. You can also use the time to familiarize her to your home and to explain some of the things you'd like her to do when she watches your child.

* Verbally prepare your child before the babysitter comes. Explain that you will be out and that he will be spending time with the babysitter. Kids can understand more than you think, and telling them in advance helps them to emotionally prepare. Be sure to include all of the fun things he'll be able to do with the sitter!

* Give your babysitter license to be extra fun. We want our kids to *love* our sitter, so we encourage her to do fun things with them like watching extra TV shows and giving them treats. This works so well that our daughter sometimes *asks* us to leave, just so she can spend time with the babysitter. Talk about an easy exit for us!

The Magic Touch

Houdini escaped from a straitjacket while dangling upside down from the roof of a building. David Copperfield walked through the Great Wall of China. And Criss Angel somehow managed to steal one of Hugh Hefner's girlfriends.

But for tons of parents just like you, the most impressive magic trick anybody could ever come up with would be one that actually lets you stay *one step ahead* of your increasingly savvy toddler.

Ladies and gentlemen, is *this* the experiment you were thinking of?

Age	Ability Tested
12–18 months	Problem Solving

What You Need

☞ a burp cloth

☞ a toy small enough that it can be easily covered up by your hand

☞ a kid who is no longer fooled by the "magic tricks" you pulled in Experiments #9 or #10

☞ maybe a teensy tiny bit of sleight-of-hand skills, if you've got them

How It Works

1. Lay the burp cloth out flat right in front of your child, so it's easily within her reach.

2. Show your child the toy and get her interested in it. You can even let her hold it for a second or two, if that helps capture her attention.

3. Take the toy and place it on the table in front of you.

4. While your child is watching, cover the toy with your hand so it is totally hidden from view.

5. Slide your hand (with the toy beneath it) all the way under the burp cloth until it's completely covered.

6. Sneakily let go of the toy and leave it under the burp cloth as you slide your hand back into view—but keep your hand in the same position as before, so your child can't tell that the toy is no longer under your hand.

7. Turn your hand over to show your child your empty hand. (Go ahead and throw in a little magician's finger flair or eyebrow raise if you're feeling it.)

8. Watch what your child does.

So there you have it.

Over the past several months, you've watched your little one figure out every object disappearing act you've thrown at her. She found your keys under one burp cloth. Then she eventually located your phone under the second burp cloth. But at least for now, your stuff is safe—it looks like you've got her stumped again.

Even though your kid understands that objects are permanent even when they're out of view, and despite the fact that she no longer makes

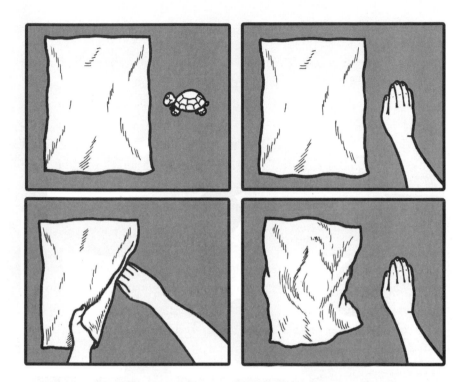

the error of focusing only on a single hiding spot anymore, she still probably never even thought to look under the burp cloth for the toy after she didn't find it in your hand. Which seems especially crazy to us adults, since the bulge of the toy under the cloth was clearly visible the whole time!

It may be second nature to us, but the thought process required to figure out this trick is brand new for our kids. Although they began to develop object permanence several months ago, it's not until about eighteen months old that most children can pass the most complex object permanence tasks like this one. To do so, children must be able to hold the image of the object in mind so well that they can keep track of it despite not being able to see it as it moves multiple times.

So just in case you were thinking about it, *do not* let your miniscule little mark bet her college fund on a back-alley game of three-card monte just yet. There's no way she's finding the red queen anytime soon.

Tips to Help Your Child

This experiment is a good demonstration of your kid's ability to identify a problem (needing to find the hidden toy) and taking steps to solve it (looking under your hand—and if it isn't there, looking under the burp cloth).

In the coming years, you'll be instrumental in helping your child develop problem-solving skills during all sorts of activities, like playing games, doing homework, studying for a test, managing allowance money, and lots more. Here are some things to keep in mind that can help you be helpful to her:

* *Constantly monitor her understanding, being sensitive to her changing level of knowledge.* This means giving her more independence and fewer directions when you sense she's capable enough on her own, while providing extra support when you sense she really needs it.

* *Explicitly discuss your own thinking and strategy use with your kid.* For example, tell her how *you* thought through a problem to get a solution, how you realized you weren't going to remember a phone number so you wrote it down to refer to later, or how you try to quiz yourself when you're studying. Not only will this help your child learn the specific skill you happen to be discussing, but it will also help her be more aware of her own mental processes (or the way that *she* thinks) in general.

* *Encourage your child to provide her own explanations.* Research shows that when students use their own words to explain example problems or text they have just read, it helps them to internalize the information and perform better when tested.

Tips to Help Yourself

If you happened to be a total childhood magic geek like *one* of the authors of this book (we're not saying which one . . . oh, yes we are—it was Andy), don't put your magic wand away too quickly. Your kid may stop falling for *this* particular illusion soon, but rest assured that you will still be able to dazzle her with your amateur magician antics for quite a few years to come.

Research suggests that kids believe magic tricks—like cutting and reassembling a rope, producing a rabbit out of a hat, or balancing the federal budget—are *really magical* until they're about five years old. After that, they figure out that they're just tricks, but they still think they're pretty cool. At least until everybody at school decides magic is totally lame, and your kid never wants to watch your famous cups and balls routine again.

Sigh.

That cups and balls routine was really good, too.

Talk to the Hand

Quick, show us your favorite gesture!

Whoa. That was pretty dirty. Do you bathe your baby with those hands?

So although the idea of gesturing has apparently gotten raunchy for old folks like us, it's a completely different story for our kids.

Try this observational experiment out on your sweet little innocent angel baby and you'll be able to see how much he gestures already, how his gestures can predict his upcoming language development milestones, and how you can use gesture to help increase his ever-growing vocabulary!

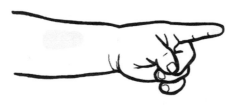

Age	Ability Tested
12–24 months	Language Development

What You Need

☞ your kid

☞ your eyeballs

☞ a clear line of sight between your kid and your eyeballs

How It Works

Because this is an observational experiment, there isn't any extra equipment or special setup required. You just need to watch your child during your regular, everyday interactions, taking note of each of the following:

1. *Which objects does your child gesture toward?* Any type of gesture counts, including pointing at an object, reaching with an open hand toward something, holding an object in his hand and extending it out to show you, and so forth.

2. *How often does he gesture toward objects?* Pay particular attention if he starts gesturing more than usual.

3. *Does your child ever gesture and say a word at the same time?* This could be any word paired with any gesture. For example, he could say "milk" and point at a bottle, say "Daddy" and motion toward a chair, or say "Macarena" and start doing the Boot Scootin' Boogie (although that would be a pretty embarrassing mistake for him, right?).

So what did you notice? Probably that your child already does a lot more gesturing than you realized! Motioning with your hands is such a natural part of development that even blind children do it—despite the fact that they can't see other people gesture, see themselves gesture, or see what effect their gestures have on an audience.

That's because gestures are not just meaningless motions meant to keep your hands busy while your mouth is gabbing away. They actually have very important connections to the way you think, speak, and communicate. Just consider how informative your own child's gestures are. Without him saying a word, you could look at the way he was moving his hands and tell pretty easily whether he wanted you to give him a bottle, or get it out of his face.

One of the reasons your kid is so good at getting his point across through gesture is that he's been practicing it for a long time. Because hands are easier to control than vocal chords, babies start communicating with gestures well before they're able to do the same thing using speech. Kids point before they say their first words, and they combine gestures with a single word before they can combine multiple words into sentences. Throughout development, what your kid's hands are doing *now* shows you what his mouth will be doing *next*.

Which is exactly what those three things you were supposed to look for during this experiment were all about.

First, we told you to pay attention to *which objects* your child gestures toward—because those are most likely the words he will be saying soon. The objects of children's gestures tend to be the words that make up the majority of their early vocabulary.

We also told you to pay attention to *how often* he gestures toward objects—because that is an indicator of how big your child's early vocabulary will be. The more objects your child gestures toward, the closer he is to learning a bunch of new words.

Finally, we asked you to pay attention to when your child gestures *and says a word at the same time*—because that means he's getting close to being able to combine two spoken words together, creating his first basic sentences. So if your kid says "Daddy" while pointing to a chair, pretty soon he'll be saying, "Daddy, sit." And if he points to his mouth while saying "Kitty," it means he intends to eat your cat.

So seriously, keep him away from the cat.

Tips to Help Your Child

Use *your* gestures! (Excluding the dirty ones, of course.) Research shows that kids with parents who gesture more have larger vocabularies. (They probably also have more accidental eye-pokings to deal with—but that seems like an acceptable trade-off if you ask us.)

Not only do children learn from the specific gestures you produce, but seeing you gesture a lot encourages *them* to gesture more too—which, as this experiment showed, bodes well for their growing vocabularies.

A major reason children who gesture more tend to learn more words is *you*. When kids gesture it encourages their parents to talk. For example, if your ravenous rascal gestures toward an apple with an opening-and-closing hand, you're likely to respond by saying something like, "Apple? You want an apple?" If he nods his head and continues motioning with his hands at this point, you're more likely to continue. "Yes, apple. You like apples. Let me peel the skin off the apple first." See what he did there? Just by gesturing, he made you talk. And talk. And talk. And talk. And the more you talked, the more language he learned.

Here are some suggestions for incorporating more gestures into your day:

* **Use gestures when talking about objects.** Pointing to an object you're referring to or holding it up to show him while you're talking about it can help your child learn its name.

* **Use gestures when talking about actions.** Pantomiming actions while you're talking about them can help your child understand what verbs mean. Unlike nouns, verbs aren't always present and touchable (for example, a "jump" is only here for the split second you're doing it, but a stuffed panda can sit in the corner staring at you all day)—so verbs tend to be harder for kids to learn.

* **Use gestures while reading books.** Gesturing toward pictures in a book can help your child understand how the words he's hearing relate to things he's seeing. Pointing to a character while you say its name or pantomiming actions as they happen verbally can help him learn words and understand the story. And running your fingers along the text while you're reading can help him learn that those squiggly lines and letters are actually meaningful.

✳ ***Sing songs that include gestures.*** Whether they involve spiders, bus wheels, or knees and toes, these are just fun. Plus, getting your child's hands moving may lead to him producing more gestures, both in and out of song.

Tips to Help Yourself

Research has shown that kids learn and remember things better when they, or their teachers, gesture during a lesson.

So the next time you find yourself needing to instruct your little one on something you'd *really* like him to remember—like, say, that toilet water is *not* for drinking—don't merely rely on your words to get the message across. Push that potty away with your hands, grimace and gag and rub that taste off of your tongue, stomp around, wail and moan, and make the yuckiest yuck faces your kid has ever seen.

And maybe, just maybe, he won't do the same thing tomorrow.

Monkey See

Kids are full of surprises.

Whether they're figuring out how to take their diapers off all by themselves, informing you that if they could be any animal in the whole world they would be a Pegasus, or shaving off large chunks of the family dog's fur, a big part of being a parent involves turning around, seeing something totally shocking, and wondering, *where in the world are they coming up with this stuff?*

As this experiment will show you, they actually learn a lot of it by watching you!

Age	Abilities Tested
14–18 months	Social Development, Learning, Memory

What You Need

- ☞ an object that your child has never seen before that is safe enough for her to handle (so no chainsaws, please)

- ☞ an idea for a truly unique way to interact with this object— it can't be an action your kid might do with the object by chance, and it shouldn't be something she has seen people do with objects before

Here are a few examples of the types of things that can work:

* An avocado, kumquat, or other fruit or vegetable your child doesn't know rolled between your feet

* A strange-looking tool or office supply you bring home from work and stick in your armpit

* An obscure kitchen utensil you tap with your elbow

* Any new cause-and-effect toy—you know, one of those gadgets that lets you push a button, flip a switch, or pull a lever to make it light up, buzz, play music, or do some other totally annoying thing that makes you want to smash it into bits and toss it in the garbage every time your kid goes to sleep—demonstrated in a strange and unusual way

How It Works

1. Choose the new object you plan to share with your child, and practice your silly way of interacting with it in private a couple of times until you're comfortable with it.

2. With the object in hand, sit down across from your kid, making sure you're more than an arm's length away from her (so she can't grab the thing too early).

3. Get your baby's attention, saying something like, "Look at this! Look what I'm doing!"

4. Once you're sure your child is watching you, demonstrate your nonsensical way of using the new object three times.

Feel free to continue saying, "Look at me! Look at me!" the whole time, as if you were some wannabe celebrity desperate to get your own reality TV show, because it's important to keep your kid's attention throughout this entire step.

5. Immediately distract your baby with something else and stash the new object, so she's unable to see or play with it for a while.

6. Wait at least fifteen minutes, then take out the new object, put it in front of your baby, and invite her to play with it.

7. Watch what she does.

Your little monkey has been able to ape things like facial expressions pretty much since the day she was born. But what you watched in *this* experiment wasn't just simple imitation. By making your child wait to play with the toy, and then seeing her copy your bizarre interaction with it at a later time, you witnessed a trick your kid is only now starting to figure out—*deferred imitation*.

Deferred imitation requires your child to watch you do something, hold it in her mind, and then perform it at a later time when you are no longer demonstrating it. Your child exhibited deferred imitation in this experiment, but she probably does it in other everyday situations as well. Have you ever seen her grab your car keys, clomp around in your oversized shoes, and try to escape out the front door? She's mimicking the way she sees you leave the house every day. If she's ever greeted Grandma with a warm, rousing "WTF, buddy!"—perhaps it's because of something *you* said in traffic on the way over there.

Adding this element of memory to plain old imitation is a pretty impressive feat for a child as young as yours. What's even more amazing? The researchers who created this experiment found that your baby can actually hold the action to be imitated in her mind for much longer than you made her wait. One study showed that after waiting an entire week between seeing the action and being able to play with the toy, fourteen-month-olds *still* imitated what they saw so very long ago.

On the other hand, you may have tried this experiment only to find that your child didn't imitate you at all!

If that's the case, don't worry. Your kid may just need another month or so to reach this particular point in her development. Or maybe she'll just never be much of a copycat. Research shows that there are considerable individual differences in children's deferred imitation—some kids tend to imitate a lot, and others do so very little. And these differences tend to remain stable over time. So maybe you have a child who keenly observed your actions and imitated them to a T, or maybe you have a child who keenly observed you looking like a complete weirdo and decided not to follow suit.

Either way, it's important to realize that whether she mimics you or not, your child does naturally learn through imitation. And she's observing you, and learning from you, all the time—even when you're not trying to teach her anything!

Tips to Help Your Child

Everybody wants their kids to do well in school, right? And learning to read and write is obviously a huge part of that. So as you work to give your studious little shorty a leg up in the literacy skills department, remember there's more than one way to teach her what she needs to know.

You can certainly use techniques involving direct instruction, like reading with your child, teaching her about letter names and sounds, practicing writing letters and lots of other activities like that. But there's another teaching method you may not have thought of and which takes advantage of your child's natural tendency to imitate: seeing *you* read and enjoy books.

Because parents are powerful role models for kids (even when they're not trying to be), seeing you read a book for pleasure, use a cookbook, or refer to a user manual for instructions on how to untangle a stuffed bunny rabbit's ears after they get caught in that spinning thing at the bottom of the dishwasher can be really powerful. It communicates that books are not just a baby thing to be dismissed when you're big enough to do other things with your time.

Simply *having* books and other reading materials in your home can promote children's literacy skills. If these materials are readily available, children are more likely to use them. So make sure there's plenty of stuff to read in multiple places around your house. And then model using them yourself!

(The fact that you're reading this book right now is a great start!)

Tips to Help Yourself

Unless you have some perverse desire to keep hunching over and picking up after the never-ending toy tornado that is your child for the rest of her juvenile life, you're going to want to encourage her to clean up after herself as soon as possible.

So use a combination of direct instruction ("OK, everybody! It's cleanup time!" or "Here's how we use the dustpan!") and modeling behavior (let her *see* you wash the dishes and vacuum the carpet, plus try to keep *your* room as clean as you'd like hers to be), and hopefully, someday, with a little bit of luck, your home might not look like a total disaster area anymore.

That's Why There's Broccoli and Vanilla

We're not sure who first said "variety is the spice of life." But we're pretty sure it wasn't a one-year-old. Little kids like what they like, and they have no problem telling you when they *don't* like what you're giving them for dinner.

And because they're so little, they haven't yet learned that other people sometimes like different things than they do.

But then one day, they start figuring it out. Do this experiment twice—once when your kid is about fourteen months old and again about four months after that—and you can find out exactly when that happens!

Age	Ability Tested
14–18 months	Social Development

What You Need
- ☛ one bowl of a food you know your child will like—fishy crackers fit the bill in our house
- ☛ one bowl of a food you know your child will *not* like—wasabi peas, anyone?
- ☛ a tray big enough to hold both bowls side by side

How It Works

Before you actually start the experiment, put the two bowls of food out for your kid to see, and invite her to snack on them a bit while she's playing. You don't have to make sure she tastes both foods or anything—just give her the opportunity to satisfy her curiosity (or rumbly tummy) now, so it won't be a distraction later.

1. Sit across from your child at a table. She can be in a high chair or on another person's lap.

2. Put the tray containing the two bowls of food in front of you, out of your child's reach.

3. Taste the food that is *undesirable* to your child, making big, obvious, over-the-top happy facial expressions and sound effects to show your kid just how much you *love* it. As you are eating, say: "Mmmm! Peas! Mmmm! I tasted the peas! Mmmm mmm mmm mmm mmmm!"

4. Now taste the food that is *desirable* to your child, making big, obvious, over-the-top unhappy facial expressions and sound effects to show how much you *hate* it. As you are eating, say: "Eww! Crackers! Eww! I tasted the crackers! Eww, yuck! Eww, eww, blech!"

5. Place one hand—palm facing up—exactly midway between the two bowls. Ask your child, "Can you give me some?" and then slide the tray toward her. If she picks one of the snacks and hands it to you, congrats! This experiment's finished! If

she doesn't hand you anything right away, keep asking until she does. (Just make sure that if she starts eating the food herself, you pull your hand back and wait until she has no food in her hands or mouth, and is not reaching toward a bowl already, before you ask again.)

Let's recap what just happened, shall we? You fixed yourself and your snacking buddy two different foods to munch on. You tasted them both right in front of her, making it *ridiculously obvious* that you loved one food and despised the other. Then you asked her to hand you something to eat, and which one did she offer?

Well, if you did this experiment with a fourteen-month-old, she most likely gave you the food you just told her you hated! And she probably did it with a smile, too! What kind of two-faced, passive-aggressive, already-fully-prepared-to-join-a-high-school-clique power game is your kid playing here?

Actually, it's not that at all.

By giving you the food you said tasted gross earlier, your child was actually being very sweet. After all, that's the food that *she* likes. And at this age, she can't separate what she likes from what you or anybody else does.

Which is why this experiment gets *really* interesting when you repeat it just four months later. After your kid hits a year and a half of age, chances are good she'll behave quite differently—and actually decide to hand you the food you said you liked! Your child's ability to override her own distaste for your preferred snack and give it to you anyway shows that she's beginning to understand something about other people's minds. She realizes now that other people can have different desires than she does, and she can infer what your desires are based on the happy and unhappy emotions you expressed.

That's pretty impressive for a child so young, considering how difficult the concept that other people have different thoughts, feelings, and beliefs remains for kids across the next few years of development. It's not until kids are about five years old that they understand this and act accordingly across most situations. (Heck, it's even difficult for adults to understand sometimes. Just ask anybody in Congress.)

Tips to Help Your Child

Even though this experiment showed that your kid is capable of compassion on a very basic level, her development in this area still has a long way to go. So don't be surprised if she struggles to imagine herself in someone else's shoes when more complex, real-life conflicts come up. Like sharing.

One reason sharing is so hard for young kids is that they simply can't see the situation from another child's perspective. So appeals like "be nice" and "you would be upset if someone did that to you" don't have as much meaning to your youngster as they do to you.

When your child is still a toddler, the easiest way to deal with inevitable sharing issues is to distract her. Just shift her focus with some tickles on the tummy or swinging-upside-down shenanigans, show her a different toy she might rather play with, offer to read her a book, or ply her with a snack.

But as your child gets older, you can start using routine spats as learning opportunities. By the time your child is preschool aged, start using these problem-solving steps to help resolve isolated sharing issues and to promote your child's skills in solving her own problems in the future:

* *Always take the object of the conflict away.* This neutralizes the object while the issue is being resolved.

* *Ask the children what's going on*—not so you can assign blame but so everyone feels like they're being heard.

* *Acknowledge the children's feelings by naming them out loud:* "It looks like you're mad that she took the toy from you," or "You seem really upset." We know this might sound touchy-feely and unnecessary, but kids feel better after they know you have heard and understood them. This can help diffuse the situation so you can resolve the problem.

* *Ask the kids how they think this problem could be resolved.* Kids are often better at this than you would imagine, generating solutions they find agreeable and that you might never have thought of. Or even better, by the time you reach this step, they may have gotten over the whole thing and moved on to something else. Which means you can, too. (Now where's that margarita machine?)

Tips to Help Yourself

Want to make addressing issues (sharing or otherwise) even less of a fight for you? Try giving your kid exactly what she wants—*in wish form*. Here's an actual example from a conversation we had with our three-year-old daughter who was approaching freak-out mode when we told her she couldn't sleep in our bed with us:

"I know how much you want to sleep with Mommy and Daddy. If I could have any wish in the whole wide world, I would wish for a giant bed as big as our whole room so that we could all sleep in it together," Amber said, feigning utmost sincerity.

"But Mommy and I don't have any wishes," added Andy, obviously feigning great disappointment, "so our bed is only big enough for Mommy and Daddy."

This seems like it would never work. But it did. We know—crazy, right? We can hardly believe it ourselves, and we were there.

But notice that before we made our wish, we let her know that we *understood* how much she really wanted it. Kids want to feel listened to, understood, and supported. And this strategy works because feeling like somebody really "gets you" is often more important than any other thing a child may have originally thought she wanted.

School Belt

Tools are pretty great inventions. They let you silence squeaks, dry up drips, and remove batteries from migraine-inducing musical toys.

Using tools is also an excellent way to build motor and problem-solving skills in kids (once they're coordinated enough to use them without maiming themselves, that is).

This experiment gives you an informative look into how your kid's ability to use tools develops—along with one really good reason why Junior shouldn't be allowed to play with a nail gun anytime soon.

Age	**Abilities Tested**
14–24 months	Motor Skills, Problem Solving

What You Need

- ☞ a spoon
- ☞ your kid's food
- ☞ a hairbrush
- ☞ your kid's hair
- ☞ something your kid could feed with a spoon or brush with a hairbrush—like a puppet, doll, stuffed animal, or sibling

How It Works

For this experiment, you'll be following the same basic procedure several times, allowing you to notice differences in how your child uses tools depending on whether he's directing them toward himself or toward others. You should sit your child in a comfortable yet contained location, like in a high chair or on another adult's lap, and make sure you have his attention before starting each task.

☞ SELF-DIRECTED SPOON TASK

1. Holding the spoon as you normally would, say, "Watch what we do with this!" and feed your child a bite of food.

2. Load the spoon up with another bite of food and say, "Now it's your turn to try."

3. Holding the spoon between your thumb and index finger instead of your normal spoon grip (so you don't bias your child's grip behavior), hand it to your child and allow him to feed himself a bite.

4. Watch your child's behavior carefully. How well does he use the spoon? Does he have to readjust his grip, or does he grab it correctly right away? How quickly and efficiently does he seem to be able to complete the action?

☛ OTHER-DIRECTED SPOON TASK

1. Holding the spoon as you normally would, say, "Watch what we do with this!" and pretend to feed an imaginary bite of food to the puppet, doll, stuffed animal, or sibling.

2. Pretend to scoop up a new bite of food and say, "Now it's your turn to try."

3. Holding the spoon between your thumb and index finger, hand it to your child, and allow him to pretend feeding the puppet.

4. Watch your child's behavior carefully, just like before.

☛ SELF-DIRECTED HAIRBRUSH TASK

1. Holding the hairbrush as you normally would, say, "Watch what we do with this!" and demonstrate brushing your hair.

2. Finish brushing and say, "Now it's your turn to try."

3. Holding the brush between your thumb and index finger instead of your normal hairbrush grip, hand it to your child and allow him to brush his own hair.

4. Watch your child's behavior carefully. How well does he use the hairbrush? Does he have to readjust his grip, or does he

grab it correctly right away? How quickly and efficiently does he seem to be able to complete the action?

☛ OTHER-DIRECTED HAIRBRUSH TASK

1. Holding the hairbrush as you normally would, say, "Watch what we do with this!" and pretend to brush the puppet's hair.

2. Finish brushing and say, "Now it's your turn to try."

3. Holding the brush between your thumb and index finger, hand it to your child and allow him to pretend brushing the puppet's hair.

4. Watch your child's behavior carefully, just like before.

So whether your tiny tool handler was spooning or brushing, did you notice a pattern here? Odds are, your kid had an easier time using the tools when they were directed toward *himself* rather than toward *others*. His movements were probably quicker, more efficient, and required fewer adjustments to his grip on the tool to complete.

Using a tool requires a person to mentally construct an action plan for how it will be used. When you can see that plan in your mind, you'll know how to pick up the tool correctly the first time you touch it. Because your child made fewer grip adjustments when he used the tools on himself, it shows he was better able to mentally construct an action plan for using the tools on himself.

(So seriously, nail guns, hacksaws, and superglue within your toddler's reach? Not a good idea.)

This experiment shows that your child is already a proficient little problem-solver. You watched him keep an end goal in mind, formulate a plan to achieve it, and figure out how to use the tool to get it done. It just so happens that he's initially better at doing this when he's focused on himself rather than on something else.

And this difference will probably get even more pronounced over the next few years. As he gains experience using utensils and personal grooming products directed toward himself, these actions will become more and more automated. He won't even have to *think* about how he picks up a brush pretty soon, because he will be so practiced at brushing his own hair. So doing these actions for someone else may *always* pose a bigger challenge.

If you've ever zoned out and forgotten whether you put on deodorant or not, and then turned around and bumbled your way through a messy attempt to do your child's hair, you know exactly what we mean.

Tips to Help Your Child

If you're looking for a fun way to help boost your kid's problem-solving skills, take a quick look in his toy box.

One research study showed that kids who engage in more complex and exploratory play—including *combining* different toys and discovering new uses for objects—are able to solve problems more quickly. This study also showed that boys tended to engage in more advanced object-oriented play and perform better overall than girls.

But this gender difference doesn't mean boys are naturally better at solving problems than girls. Instead, it points to differences in the ways that boys and girls regularly use toys. Boys are more likely than girls to have open-ended and constructive toys like blocks and balls in their play areas, and they tend to use them in more diverse ways. This extra experience boys get matters because it influences their ability to use tools to solve problems.

So having fun and flexible toys in the house, making them readily available to your child, and playing with them together can encourage more sophisticated object play and promote your child's problem-solving skills—regardless of his or her gender!

Tips to Help Yourself

Think this experiment was all about studying your child's first attempts to use tools?

Think again.

Your kid is already a complete expert at using one great big tool: *you*. (That's right. Your one-year-old just called you a tool. What are you gonna do about it?)

You are your child's first tool—and he's been using you as such since he was about six months old. Right now he uses you to help him open a package of fruit snacks or tell him what all those words in his favorite books say. Later on, it'll be for gas money, a place to crash while he's "finding himself" after college, and eventually free babysitting for your grandkids.

So do yourself a favor and relish the times you get to act as his tool now—because this is about as painless as it's going to get!

Getting Into Shapes

I f you're like most parents, you haven't had very much "taking care of me" time since the baby came along. You fuss less about the hairs on your head and often forget about trimming the ones in your nose. You rarely sleep in and almost never work out.

This experiment won't help you with any of that.

But what it *will* do is give your *kid* an intense word-learning workout that will enable her to learn a bunch of words every day! By following these simple steps multiple times over the next several weeks, you won't just be teaching your munchkin words—you'll be teaching her *how to learn* them!

Age	Ability Tested
14–24 months	Language Development

What You Need

☛ a pair of objects that are clearly the same shape but are different in as many other ways as possible (like size, color, material, and texture)

  Good example: a small, blue, plastic fork paired with a large, silver serving fork

☛ 3 additional pairs of objects selected in the same way—two balls, two cups, two blocks, etc.

☛ 4 other toys or household objects, which can be anything you want as long as they are *not* one of the things you chose to be an object pair

How It Works

1. Set up a normal, everyday play situation for you and your child. You could both be sitting on the floor or at the table in a chair and high chair.

2. Take out one of your specially designed object pairs (let's say it's the forks) and play with them for five minutes in the same ways you usually play with toys—except during this experiment, make sure to name the objects at least ten times while you're playing.

    Here are some ideas for fun ways to do it:

    * Pass the objects to each other ("Here are the *forks*! Can you hand the *forks* back to Daddy?")

    * Hide the objects behind your back and dramatically take them out again ("Where are the *forks*? Oh, here they are!")

    * Pretend with the objects by making them fly ("The *forks* are flying!"), or walk across the table ("Aaaahhh! The *forks* are alive!")

    * Use the objects in conjunction with other toys ("The *forks* are riding in the wagon.")

    * Put the objects in funny places ("I have a *fork* nose!")

    * Or anything else you can imagine! The possibilities are endless!

3. Halfway through your play session, bring out one of your other, nonpaired toys or household objects. Show it to your child, point out that it is *not* the same as the objects you've been playing with ("This is *not* a fork!"), then put it away and

continue playing with your object pair until the five minutes are up.

4.   Repeat steps 2 and 3 three more times, until you've played for five minutes with each of your four pairs of objects. And don't feel like you have to do all the pairs back to back—this experiment still works even if you spread the play out over time.

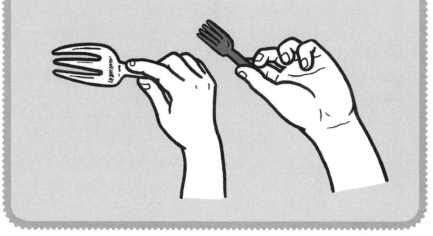

OK, all you type A, achievement-minded supermoms and dads out there. You just learned a way to help your kid start boning up for the SATs—and you haven't even potty trained her yet! (Or *have* you? Man, you people are intense!)

For best results, you'll want to repeat this experiment multiple times over the next several weeks. Since you can incorporate it into regular play, it should be pretty easy to do. The only hurdle will be getting your broken-by-parenthood brain to remember to do it.

So how does this experiment teach your child to learn words? Well, it's actually pretty simple. When you call two things by the same name—"fork" for instance—your child instinctively tries to identify what it is that makes both of these things "forks." In other words, she's looking for how the objects are *similar*. In this experiment, you made that task really easy because you showed her two forks that are *different* in almost every way—*except shape*. So she learns "forks" are fork-shaped.

At the same time, she's learning about three other pairs of objects (like balls, cups, and blocks), which this experiment soon teaches her are *also* named for their shapes. That's right, people. "Balls" are ball-shaped, "cups" are cup-shaped, and "blocks" are block-shaped. When she puts all of this experience together, she learns the general rule that "BLANKs are BLANK-shaped," or that objects are named for their shape.

And just like that, your little egghead knows exactly what she needs to pay attention to when learning an object's name!

After you've given your kid this important word-learning lesson, you can expect to see some pretty impressive results. Not only will she learn the trained words faster than she would have otherwise, but she will probably start to learn words you haven't even trained her on more quickly too. The result? Her everyday vocabulary will begin growing by leaps and bounds, and before long she'll be totally ready for those college entrance exams—about a decade and a half early!

Tips to Help Your Child

Another aspect of this experiment that makes it so effective for teaching your child is that it uses comparison and contrast. Your child *compared* a pair of similarly named objects to learn what was alike about them, and she *contrasted* them against an object with a different name that you brought out midway through each play session to see what it was that distinguished them.

Using these two techniques can help kids learn more stuff much faster.

For example, if you and your child had played with the small, blue, plastic fork one day and then played with the large, silver serving fork on another day, she would still learn about forks. But it would take her longer to realize that "forks" are fork-shaped, because you never narrowed her focus onto the details that were most relevant. Instead of being clued in really quickly to the idea that shape was ultraimportant for naming, your child would have to keep in mind *all* the different experiences with forks she'd been amassing over time, and then attempt to analyze for herself what was the same and different about each of them.

Research has shown that comparison and contrast can help kids learn all kinds of new things, including nouns, adjectives, how to solve math problems, and how to use analogies (just to name a few). So it's smart to incorporate comparison and contrast into everyday play situations with your child. If you're trying to teach your child about sizes, you could compare a small chair and a small mouse, saying, "Look, these are both little!" You could also contrast things that are different only in the feature you are trying to teach. Show her a big cup and a little cup, saying, "This one is big and this one is little." Apply this idea to help your child learn anything, from the nouns she'll be learning tomorrow to the calculus problems she'll be learning way too soon!

Tips to Help Yourself

Now that your kid is getting the hang of comparison and contrast, *you* could be getting a brand-new way to keep her occupied whenever you need a few precious minutes to yourself. The next time your little one just won't leave you alone while you're trying to rest your eyes for a second, pay a utility bill, or have a conversation with an actual adult, try this:

Look at whatever toy, book, personal grooming device, or piece of garbage she's brought to show you and say, "Oh wow! You found a BLANK! Can you go find *another* BLANK?" Her enthusiasm for her newfound comparison abilities will send her off happily to find you a match, during which time *you* can go back to what you were doing.

When she returns in triumph, celebrate her accomplishment for a moment, then use *contrast* to send her on her next mission, saying something like, "You have a green BLANK! Can you go get a pink BLANK now?" Boo-yah. Just like that, more "me" time is yours.

Keep up this game of fetch as long as you want. After all, it's good for her vocabulary—and great for your sanity!

Quick Learner

In the last experiment, you discovered an effective technique for nurturing every last ounce of word-learning potential out of your baby's brain. Odds are by now, he's gotten pretty darn good at it. And he's about to get even better.

This experiment takes a look at how a simple exercise in counting lets you know when your budding babbler will be able to start learning brand-new words *immediately*.

Age	Ability Tested
15–24 months	Language Development

What You Need

☛ For Part 1: your favorite way to take notes (pencil and paper, computer and note-taking app, crayon and whatever crumpled-up scrap of paper you can find in the den of chaos your child has reduced your home to, etc.)

☛ For Part 2: a set of four specially selected objects from around the house (Read page 110 for more details.)

How It Works

☞ **PART 1**

1. Figure out the number of words your child has spoken to date. The words don't have to have been perfectly pronounced to make your list. It's totally normal for some words to sound like a single syllable from the word (like "duh" for *duck* or "buh" for *banana*), a repetition of a single syllable of the word (like "baba" for *bottle*) or a mouth fart (like "pfffttt" for *photosynthesis*). For this list, anything your child intended to be a word should count.

For some of you, quantifying your child's vocabulary will be easier than for others. If you're like us (or just Amber, really), you've been keeping track of every single new word your child has said via painstakingly detailed notes on a massive daily calendar. If that sounds like you, then this phase of the experiment will be really easy—just check your calendar and count up the number of words your child has said to date.

If, on the other hand, you're *not* a total language development nerd, you'll need to think back to all of the words you've heard your child say so far. We know, it sounds like an impossible task. But research shows that children's first words usually fall into several predictable categories:

* ***Proper names***—like names of family members, friends, and pets

* ***Animal names***—cat, bear, anything on Old MacDonald's farm

* ***Sound effects and animal sounds***—*vroom* for cars, *ruff ruff* for dogs, *pfffttt* for farts (only when he's *not* talking about photosynthesis)

* *Food items*—milk, grapes, organic gluten-free mac-n-cheese

* *Household items*—blanket, spoon, bowl

* *Toys*—ball, book, Mommy's phone

* *Vehicles*—car, truck, bike, Wienermobile

* *Furniture and rooms*—bed, chair, kitchen

* *Verbs*—stir, sleep, eat, poop

* *Adjectives*—big, empty, sticky, stinky

Go through each of these categories one at a time, spend some time thinking about all of the related words you might have ever heard your child use in each of them, and write them all down. (Remember, *any attempt* makes the list!) Then count up the words.

How It Works

☞ PART 2

1. Think of some small household objects you own that your child would *not* know the names of—like a headband, tongs, whisk, button, tiara, mouth guard, melon baller, spork, tweezers, nail file, rubber band, those square things that keep your bread closed, etc. Make sure they're actually things your child does *not* know the names of, so you can see if he's truly learning a word during this part of the experiment. Gather a specially selected set of four of these objects, so you have one object that fits each of the following categories:

* **Main object:** Choose a main object you will name for your child, asking him to select which other object shares the same name (example: a large, gray, metal spatula).

* **Correct option:** Choose an object to be the correct match. It should be the same type of object as the main object you selected, but it should be different in other ways like size, color, and material (example: a small, black, plastic spatula).

* **Decoy option:** Choose an object to serve as a decoy. It should match your main object in size, color, or material but should *not* match in type of object (example: a large, gray, metal whisk).

* **Additional option:** Choose any other object for your child to select from (example: a turkey baster).

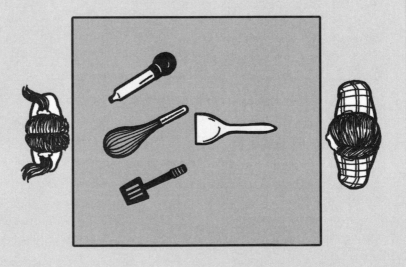

2. Sit at a table across from your child, keeping your four objects in a basket on a chair next to you, so your kid can't see them.

3. Take out the main object, place it on the table in front of your child, and name it. For example, if your main object is a large metal spatula, you'd say, "This is a spatula." NOTE: It's OK if your child touches the object, but wait until he puts it down or you can remove it from his hands (without tears of protest) before moving on to the next step. If more than a few seconds elapse before you are able to do that, name the object again—"It's a spatula."

4. Simultaneously take out all three of the other objects and place them in a row in front of your child. The main object should still be out and in your child's view, but the three options should be closest to your child.

5. Ask your kid to identify which object has the same name as the main object. In our example, you'd say, "Can you hand me the other spatula?"

6. Watch which object your child chooses—by touching it, pointing to it, picking it up, or just looking at it more than the others.

We know what you're thinking:

Hey, wait a minute! Those two phases had nothing to do with each other! Either you've totally lost your minds, or you had me count all my kid's words just to keep me busy—kind of like when I let my kid watch an extra-long cartoon so Mommy and Daddy can go into the bedroom for a little "grown-up" time!

First of all, congratulations on figuring out how to maintain some semblance of a sex life these days. And second of all, those two seemingly dissimilar activities *were* actually related! Researchers have found a relationship between the number of words in a child's vocabulary (which you figured out in Part 1) and his ability to learn a new word (which you tested in Part 2).

For many children, there seems to be something magical about having at least fifty words in their vocabulary. Before a child learns fifty words, he tends to add new words to his repertoire really slowly. A kid will say one new word, and several days—or even weeks—might pass before he says another. If during Part 1 you determined that your child had said less than fifty words, he was probably less successful at picking the correct option when you taught him a new word in Part 2.

Once your child's vocabulary hits that fifty-word threshold, however, he has basically learned how to learn words—and he is now able to learn them much more quickly. Pay attention, and you may even notice the little genius saying multiple new words per day. This newfound ability is what psychologists call a *word spurt*. And a *naming boom*. And sometimes a *vocabulary explosion*. Pretty much any phrase that means "a meaningful unit of language sounds" plus "a sudden noisy release of energy" ought to do. Here are a few more names for it that we just made up: *utterance inferno, vocalization detonation, chat barf.* So help yourself to those.

Whatever you want to call this phenomenon, it's the reason that if your child's word count was at least halfway to a hundred in Part 1, he was probably able to immediately pick the correct answer in Part 2.

And it isn't just that he can learn a word right away—he can now remember it for weeks afterward, too. He can even use the word correctly in future situations that are very different from the one in which he learned the word. Like if you point to a turtle at the zoo and call it a "turtle," your child will not only realize that specific animal is called a turtle, but he'll also be able to point out other similar animals—like a turtle at the park, a plastic toy turtle, or a picture of a turtle in a book—and know that "turtle" is the correct name for all of them.

Pretty impressive work, little chat barfer! Pretty impressive work, indeed.

Tips to Help Your Child

These days parents have an extensive mental checklist of things we feel we just *need* to start teaching our kids right away, don't we? It usually looks something like this: animal names, animal sounds (although no one knows why this one's so important anymore), shapes, colors, numbers, letters, the periodic table of the elements . . . the list goes on all the way through college.

From this list of usual suspects, colors can be particularly tough for kids to learn. A big reason is that in order to notice color, kids have to ignore all the other interesting things about an object—like how it's shaped, what it does, and how easily they can dismantle it and scatter its pieces all over your living room. That's why there's a huge age range for when kids typically learn color. Anywhere from about eighteen months to three years old is considered average.

Here are some tips for helping your child learn his colors:

* *Introduce lots of color words.* Research shows that learning colors is easier when kids are introduced to lots of different color words, rather than when adults focus on just a couple to start with.

* *Space it out.* Kids learn better when lessons are spaced out. So rather than having one long, intensive session of color discussion, spread several shorter ones out throughout your day.

* *Vary the context.* Kids learn things better when they're taught in lots of different places. Talk about color at the kitchen table, at the park, in the grocery store parking lot, and while reading a book.

* *Compare and contrast.* Compare objects of the same color and contrast them with objects that are other colors, as in, "These hot dogs are pink. But this other one is green." (P.S. Don't eat the green hot dog.)

Tips to Help Yourself

If you haven't already cleaned up that potty mouth you've been so deftly defiling since your pre-parenting days, now would be a great time to do so.

Your kid hears everything you say, you just found out that he learns everything he hears, and sooner or later, he repeats everything he learns to his preschool teacher.

Do you really want to get a phone call from school about that? H-E-double hockey sticks no, you don't!

Hey, Good Lookin'!

I f you're like most parents, you've shown your baby her reflection in the mirror a time or two. (If you're Kim Kardashian or Kanye West, your baby was almost certainly holding a compact *in utero*.)

But what does your child actually think she's seeing in that mirror? Is it a friendly neighborhood kid who just happens to show up for a playdate every time you prop your tot up on the bathroom counter? Or does she actually recognize that reflection as herself?

That's exactly what this experiment is designed to show you.

Age	Ability Tested
15–24 months	Social Development

What You Need
- ☞   a large mirror
- ☞   lipstick or face paint

How It Works

1. Without letting your child realize what you're doing, sneak a smear of lipstick onto her nose. The lipstick (or some other type of makeup or face paint if you're not a lipstick lover) should be red or a similarly dark color. In other words, it should be *totally obvious* that there's a giant smudge of color right on your kid's schnoz.

2. Plop your kid down in front of the mirror. We've found that our bathroom vanity is a great location for this experiment. But if you're the type of parent who tends to worry about your child falling from very high places onto rock-hard surfaces below, perhaps a floor mirror in a heavily carpeted room might be more up your alley.

3. Watch and see what your child does.

Your child (you know, the one whose face you just tagged like a brick wall behind a liquor store) is likely to react to this experiment in one of two ways.

First, she could *reach toward the mirror* like she's trying to touch or play with her reflection. If this happens, it shows you that your kid sees her reflection as a playmate, not as herself. This is a totally normal reaction for babies all the way up to about a year and a half old. That's because self-recognition is not something we are born with but rather an ability that develops over time.

And when that ability appears, your baby will begin reacting to this experiment in a brand-new way. Instead of reaching toward the mirror like she used to, she will now understand that the big, fat, weird-looking mark she sees on the kid's face in the mirror is actually on herself. And because she also knows by now that that mark is *not* supposed to be there, she will *reach toward her own face*—presumably to try to get that strange thing off right now!

What's pretty amazing about our self-recognition ability is that it appears to be an innate and essential part of human development. No matter who you are, what you look like, or where you live, learning to recognize your own appearance always tends to happen at about eighteen months old. Even children from cultures that do not use mirrors begin to recognize themselves at the same age.

When performing similar experiments on animals, scientists have discovered that some highly intelligent species—like dolphins and chimpanzees—are also able to recognize themselves. Less-brainy animals? Not so much. So consider it a true milestone when your baby stops reaching for the mirror and starts swiping at her nose—at that moment, your child is officially smarter than your dog!

Tips to Help Your Child

If you put your child in front of the mirror and she showed no sign of recognizing herself, you may be wondering whether you can help her realize the reflection is hers. It seems like an easy enough concept to teach, right? The reflection is doing the exact same things as your baby at the exact same times. But actually, no amount of "Look, it's you! Look, it's you!" is going to make her realize it's her own reflection in the mirror.

You also don't need to spend time trying the experiment again and again to see precisely when she realizes the reflection is hers. In fact, if you're curious about figuring out when your child may have gone from not understanding that it's her in the mirror to being ready to primp and preen with the best of them, you may do just as well simply *listening* to what she says.

The ability to recognize oneself tends to coincide with a change in a child's vocabulary. At the same time that a child develops the ability to recognize herself in the mirror and in pictures, she also tends to start using personal pronouns. So when you hear your child start to use terms like "me," "my," "mine," or "I," you may want to put her back in front of the mirror and watch—she's probably now ready to pass this test with flying colors!

As a general rule, listening to your child's vocabulary is a great way to get insight into her newly emerging skills. For example, children typically get complete object permanence around the same time they learn the related word "gone," they learn to engage in multistep problem solving when they learn the words "there" and "uh-oh," and they develop the ability to search in the middle of multiple landmarks to find an object after they learn the word "middle." So if you want to know what new developments are happening between your kid's ears, be sure to keep *your* ears open.

Tips to Help Yourself

After you're finished with this experiment, lick your thumb until it's well coated with saliva, then use it to rub your kid's face clean. After all, you're only going to have so many years until your child realizes this move is totally humiliating and completely disgusting, so you might as well take advantage now.

Yo-Yo Moppet

Before we continue, we're going to need you to go stand in front of a mirror, look yourself square in the eye, and repeat after us:

"I have a two-year-old."

It seems crazy, right? If you're anything like us, you don't know how the past twenty-four months went by so fast, yet you also can't remember what life was even like before your baby arrived.

This experiment takes you on a trip down memory lane to reminisce about how your little one has been growing surely and steadily over the past two years—while also making you realize the growth hasn't been all *that* steady after all.

Age	Ability Tested
24 months and older	Physical Development

What You Need

☛ photographs of your child—think you may have one or two of those lying around?

How It Works

1. Gather up a bunch of pictures you've taken of your little one since the day he was born. A well-organized photo album documenting his life month by month would be perfect. (Although a hard drive stuffed with a massive mess of images may be more realistic.)

2. Look through the pictures chronologically, paying close attention to periods when your child looked relatively *chubbier*—with fuller cheeks and a rounder tummy.

3. See if you can find any stretches where these chubbier photos are followed closely in time by pictures of your kid looking relatively *longer* and *leaner*.

As our first child was getting older, we noticed there were times when we would look at her and think she looked really skinny. And then there were other times when she seemed to have put on a few extra pounds. In one holiday photo, in fact, we swear our kid was sporting a *triple chin* (although at least one of those folds was a direct result of her making a completely freaked-out, I-can't-believe-I'm-sitting-right-next-to-*Santa*-at-the-mall face).

After a while we realized there was a pattern—our daughter seemed to look chubbier *just before* getting noticeably taller and thinner. It's like her little body was bottling up all of its baby fat only to suddenly churn it out in the form of a brand-new quarter-inch of height.

As it turns out, that's pretty much exactly what was happening. And it's exactly what you might have noticed while flipping through your kid's photos!

When children are going through growth spurts, it's extremely common for them to gain weight before they suddenly gain height. Because your kid has probably experienced lots of small growth spurts by the time he reaches age two, now is a great time to look back and see if you can find them.

And now that you know what to look for, you can even start observing his growth in real time to see if you can predict when he's about to get taller. Maybe then you won't be so blindsided when his shoes suddenly don't fit anymore.

Maybe.

Tips to Help Your Child

Another way to predict a growth spurt is by monitoring your child's sleep patterns. Research shows that your child needs more sleep during a growth spurt, and he will tend to snooze longer both at nighttime and naptime whenever he has one. Kind of makes you wish they'd *always* be having a growth spurt, huh?

In general, getting adequate sleep is great for children's physical growth and brain development. Sleep experts have noted that the symptoms of inadequate sleep include fatigue, irritability, decreased ability to focus attention, impaired ability to learn, and increased behavior problems. Some research suggests that too little sleep can actually mimic the symptoms of Attention Deficit Hyperactivity Disorder.

And this loss of sleep doesn't have to be huge to have a dramatic effect on your child. Researchers randomly assigned children between the ages of nine and eleven years old to go to sleep either one hour later or one hour earlier than usual for three consecutive nights. They then put the children through a series of cognitive tests. The results? The kids who slept less showed worse reaction time, memory, and learning abilities. So losing only one hour of sleep per night can actually impair kids' brains enough to interfere with school performance.

How much sleep should your child be getting? Researchers analyzed the sleep patterns of hundreds of children and found the following averages according to children's age:

Age 0: 14 hours, including 3 nap hours
Age 1: 13.5 hours, including 2 nap hours
Age 2: 13 hours, including 2 nap hours
Age 3: 12.5 hours, including 2 nap hours
Age 4: 12 hours
Age 5: 11.5 hours
Age 6: 11 hours
Age 7–8: 10.5 hours
Age 9–10: 10 hours
Age 11: 9.5 hours
Age 12–14: 9 hours
Age 15: 8.5 hours
Age 16: 8 hours

Keep in mind that there is great variability in the amount that individual children actually sleep, so don't worry too much if your child isn't following this exact pattern. Try to ensure your child is getting enough sleep by monitoring his behavior and experimenting with sleep schedules to find the right one that works for him. And once you *do* find it, stick with it. It's important that kids have a consistent bedtime, as going to bed at all different hours can disrupt children's circadian rhythms and lead to behavior problems.

If sleep is a problem in your house, try implementing a consistent bedtime routine that you do both at nighttime and naptime. Having a predictable sequence of activities before bed becomes familiar to your child and signals that it's time to relax and wind down.

In our family, bedtime for our infant includes:

* a diaper change

* kisses from Daddy and big sister

* breast-feeding and rocking with Mommy

* singing

Bedtime for our big kid includes:

* using the potty

* brushing teeth

* reading a book

* telling a story "from our minds"

* singing

Tips to Help Yourself

Although it may be tempting, please do not try to rationalize your *own* chubby cheeks and round tummy by telling people *you're* about to go through a growth spurt.

No one's going to buy it.

But they will buy the truth: you are currently raising a two-year-old, so you'll have time to start working out again in about sixteen years.

The Third Year and Beyond

Your child is getting big now, and so are his skills.

By age two he's good at lots of stuff, like running, jumping (after finally making it through the adorably long process of figuring out how to get *both* feet off the ground at once), and talking your ear off about just about anything. And he's working on even more advanced projects like doing puzzles, counting, constructing complex pretend scenarios, and honing negotiation skills that would put your local car dealer to shame.

So what might surprise you is learning about all of the things that your little genius *can't* do yet.

Sometimes all of the amazing new skills we see older children perform trick us into thinking our kids are capable of more than they actually are. That's why many of the experiments in this section are designed to stump your smarty with tests you'd think he would ace with no problem. You'll watch as your little bugsy-boo, who is normally ever so crafty at solving problems like how to con you into reading him an extra story at bedtime, is suddenly unable to complete basic tasks like figuring out whether or not he's getting his fair share of dessert.

Armed with the information these experiments give you about your child's strengths and weaknesses, you'll be better able to identify when you might be expecting too much from your child—or when he needs you to give him a gentle nudge.

Your child may be growing up, but these experiments highlight how much he still really needs you. The tips you're about to read emphasize the critical role you play in developing your child's thinking, problem solving, and academic competence. Your involvement as a parent has never been more important than it is right now, because your everyday behaviors are helping shape the kind of thinker your child will ultimately become.

And these experiments will help you set him up for success.

That's Good Enough for Me

Your kid is one smart cookie.

It seems like not a day goes by without her surprising you with something amazing and new she can do—drawing a smiley face, using the word "eventually" in a sentence, putting on her own pants.

Of course, there are other times when your kid does something so mind-numbingly moronic, you're forced to put down that pamphlet on extra-*extra*-early college admissions and remind yourself: your kid is still a kid.

This experiment is all about one of *those* times. And we should warn you right now. What your normally intelligent little imp is about to do won't merely surprise you—it's going to *totally blow your mind*.

Age	Ability Tested
2–6 years	Problem Solving

What You Need

☛ a table

☛ 3 cookies (If you can't trust yourself to gather 3 cookies without eating one, then you better make it 4 cookies.)

How It Works

1. Sit at a table across from your child.

2. Place two cookies in front of yourself and one cookie in front of your kid.

3. Ask her, "Do I have more, do you have more, or do we have the same amount?"

4. Being the genius that she is, your little one should respond that *you* have more (and that's not fair, obviously).

5. While your kid is watching you, reach across the table, pick up her cookie, break it in half, and set the two pieces back down in front of her.

6. Ask your child, "*Now do I have more, do you have more, or do we have the same amount?*"

Whoa, right? (We told you your mind would be blown.)

Even though your normally sharp little squirt watched you break her single cookie into two smaller pieces *right in front of her very own face,* she probably said that you now somehow had the same amount. And she was completely happy about it, too!

Go ahead and do a victory lap around the living room if you want to. Not only have you discovered a way to save 50 percent on your dessert expenditures for the foreseeable future, you've also got yourself a really cool new party trick. And if you want to tweak this experiment up a notch, you can. After following the directions above, reach across the table again and break your child's cookie into a *third* piece. If your kid fell for the first part of the experiment, she'll now believe that *she* has more cookie than you do—and she'll feel like she just hit the jackpot! At this exciting turn of events, our daughter Sammy actually continued to break her cookie into increasingly tiny pieces, gleefully shouting, "And more! And more!" Hey, it's not every day she gets all the dessert she wants!

Your child's reaction to this test is an extremely common one, as kids this age are easily tripped up by issues involving the quantity of objects. But why do kids make this mistake?

Well, it's actually due to *two* errors in the way kids all the way up to age seven think. First, they can only pay attention to one aspect of the situation at a time (in this case, it's the number of cookie pieces you each have), so they're unable to consider other relevant details (like the fact that her cookie halves take up considerably less space on the table than your whole cookies do). Her second error is that she fails to realize that even though an object's appearance has been changed, it still retains its essential properties—like volume.

These errors are not specific to this particular task—she would make the same two errors across a number of situations. Show her two identical glasses of water and then pour one of them into a wider, shorter container, and she will suddenly think the new container holds less water. Show her two equally sized balls of clay and then squish one into a long tube, and she will suddenly think the longer one is made up of more clay. Show her two identical rows of pennies and then spread one of them out wider on the table, and she will suddenly think the spaced-out row contains more coins—even though she could easily count them!

Over time your child will stop making these two errors, and she will become a new kind of thinker—one who can keep multiple aspects of an object in mind and use them to solve a problem. She will no longer be fooled by breaking her cookie in half because she will consider not only the number of pieces but also the overall volume they take up. She will realize an object retains its amount even when its appearance has changed. She will be a more flexible thinker who can follow her own mental logic to get to a reasoned solution.

So watch out, because at that point "because I said so" may be met by a well-thought-out, completely logical argument as to why that is actually a terribly insufficient answer. So you might want to start working on your counterargument now.

Tips to Help Your Child

After seeing your child get tricked by this experiment, you might wonder: "Can I improve her performance by teaching her to understand?" Usually, the answer to questions like this is "Nope." You can't simply teach your child a few quick lessons and expect to speed up the natural process of cognitive development. Your kid's development happens over time, and it relies on both advancing age and increasing experience with people and things in her environment.

Except that in *this* case, you *can* teach her—at least under some circumstances. Researchers have identified a critical window in which a child is open to learning through instruction. To find out if your child is in that window, do this experiment again. After your child reports whether or not you have the same amount, ask her *how she knows*. When she answers, pay attention to her gestures.

As children come to understand quantity, their speech and gestures often go through a predictable sequence:

✳ When children ***don't understand*** that an object retains its amount even when its appearance has changed, their verbal explanations and their gestures will match. For example, your child might say something like, "Because we both have two," and produce a matching gesture in which she points to her two pieces and then to your two pieces.

* When children are **on the verge of understanding** (which would probably happen at about six years old), there will be a mismatch between their verbal explanations and their gestures. For example, your child might say, "Because we both have two," but her gesture might pantomime breaking a cookie in half. In that case, her speech and her gesture say two different things entirely. Even though her words don't convey understanding about the difference between your two cookies and her one cookie, her gesture conveys an awareness that you simply broke her cookie in half.

* Finally, when children **do understand**, their verbal explanations and gestures will match again. For example, your child might say, "You have more because you just broke mine in half," and produce a matching gesture like pantomiming breaking a cookie in half.

When your child's words and gestures differ, it signals that she is in a state of transition. On some level she understands the task, even if she can't yet verbalize it. And it's at this time that she is most open to instruction. Seize the opportunity by guiding her to pay attention to *all* relevant aspects of the cookie—not just that you both have two pieces—which can help her understand that even though her cookie may look different now, it's still the exact same amount of treat. (Although for the life of us, we don't know why you'd want to do that. She's willing to eat only *half* a cookie, people! Just be happy about that and stop asking questions!)

You can also look for gesture-speech mismatches in all sorts of other, non-dessert-related problem-solving situations. It turns out that across all kinds of tasks, children tend to convey new knowledge in their gestures before they can consciously explain it. Consider these mismatches a sign that your child is ready to learn—and respond accordingly.

Tips to Help Yourself

Most kids are pretty good about eating dessert. But what about dinner? If you've got a finicky eater to contend with, make her mental errors from this experiment work for you! By changing the appearance of foods your child doesn't want to eat, you can make her think there's *less* on her plate—so it will be easier for her to get through.

If she doesn't like her milk, try pouring it into a wider cup.

If she won't stop picking at her mashed potatoes, go ahead and squish them into a new shape.

If she's putting up a stink about her peas, push them closer together.

And if she still needs some extra incentive after all that, just tell her that if she eats a good dinner, she can have two cookies for dessert! (Wink wink, nudge nudge!)

Think Inside the Box

They say being a parent is a thankless job. But that's nothing compared to what being a cartoon spokescharacter in a children's cereal commercial must be like. Whether you're a hungry rabbit being denied breakfast because it's only "for kids," or a leprechaun having your multicolored meal blatantly *stolen* from you, children never seem to treat these characters with respect.

But that might not be their fault.

With help from a simple box of cereal, this experiment shows you that your kid usually thinks only of herself because she *can't yet* think about anyone else.

Age	Ability Tested
2½–4 years	Social Development

What You Need

☛ a cereal box

☛ something unexpected to put inside the box (and remember that your kid will see it—so no severed hand Halloween decorations or sex toys please)

How It Works

1. Making sure your child is not around to see you, secretly take the bag of cereal out of the box and replace it with the unexpected object you chose. Remember, you can use anything you want as long as it's something your child would not expect to find in the box. Pencils, bouncy balls, or your high school yearbook will all do the trick.

2. Show the cereal box to your child and ask, "What do you think is in this box?" Your child should respond by saying "cereal"—if she doesn't, try a different box she might recognize better, or just head straight to the optometrist's office to get her eyes checked.

3. Empty the box to show her it's actually the unexpected object that's inside—*not* what she guessed it would be!

4. Put the unexpected object back in the box and tell her to imagine that her best friend came over. Then ask, "What do you think *your friend* would say is in the box?"

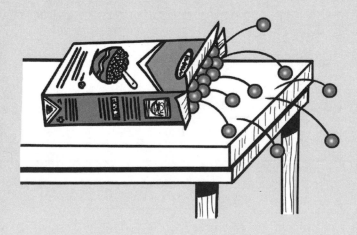

Unless your child's best friend has X-ray vision, you know full well she'd think there was cereal in that box. But that's probably not what your small fry told you, is it? Kids under four almost always report that their friends would assume the *unexpected item* to be inside the box— even though the friends had not seen the contents of the box and had no reason to think there was anything besides cereal in there. Your child responded this way because *she* knows what's inside the box, and she can't separate her own knowledge from that of her friend.

So at this point your kid can't see another person's perspective figuratively. But you know what? She can't see another person's perspective *literally* either. Researchers once set up a large, three-dimensional mountain scene so there were different things to look at on each side— like a goat and pine tree on one side and a house and a dog on the other. They let children observe the scene from each side, then had them sit on one side while an experimenter on the other side asked them questions. When the experimenter asked, "What do *you* see?" all preschoolers answered correctly, but when the experimenter asked, "What do *I* see?" children who did not yet realize that other people have a different mental experience than they do said the experimenter saw the exact same items they were currently looking at—even though they knew there was different stuff on the other side of that peak.

Young children's inability to consider another person's perspective can also be seen in their conversations. Have you ever had a chat with your child in which she seemed to start from the middle of a story, like she had a whole backstory in her mind but failed to share it with you first? Or how about when you ask her what she's been doing at preschool all day, and she just says, "I don't know" or "Nothing"? She's not doing that to blow you off. It's just that she doesn't yet realize you two have separate sets of knowledge and you don't automatically know all of the things she knows. In her mind, because *she* knows the beginning of her story and what she did at school, you must know too—so what's the point in telling you?

But somewhere between four and five years old, all of this changes, and your child will come to understand that other people have a different mental experience than she does. If you repeat this experiment then, your eensy weensy empathizer will be able to tell you that a friend who hasn't seen what's inside the cereal box would assume its contents matched what was pictured on the front—cereal! Once kids can do this, they are said to have a *theory of mind*, or the understanding that other people have their own thoughts, feelings, and beliefs.

Acquiring a theory of mind is a hugely important step in your kid's social development. Children who have mastered tasks that require insight into the mental lives of others (like this experiment) can use that knowledge to interact with people in more sophisticated and fun ways. The result? They tend to have more advanced social skills, better social adjustment, and are more highly rated by their peers. Preschool children asked to put pictures of their classmates into boxes marked with a happy face, neutral face, or sad face based on how much they liked to play with them tended to put more of their peers who had achieved a theory of mind into the happy face box.

So what your kid just learned could someday help her become president of the United States—or at least talk her way out of a speeding ticket.

Tips to Help Your Child

Children develop a theory of mind earlier when they get more practice thinking and talking about other people's thoughts and feelings. So if you want to see your kid build her skills more quickly, here are a few ways you can help:

* ✳ *Encourage pretend play.* Engaging in pretend play benefits kids' social skills because pretending requires thinking about the world from different vantage points. When children pretend to be different characters or interact with an imaginary friend, they have to consider the thoughts, experiences, and motivations of others.

* *Have family discussions about thoughts and feelings.* Talk to your child about her own feelings and guide her to think about the thoughts and feelings of other people. If you happen to see one kid push another kid at the playground, ask your child how she would feel if that ever happened to her. When reading books, talk about the thoughts and motivations that drive characters' behavior, as well as any facial expressions pictured—along with the feelings they convey.

* *Give her siblings.* Brothers and sisters spend tons of time together, and whether they're playing or fighting, they're always learning about each other's minds. Not that you can do anything about it at this point, but kids especially benefit from having an *older* sibling, since they encourage more advanced pretending, role-play, and talk about thoughts and feelings.

Tips to Help Yourself

Like playing hide-and-seek with your kid? Do yourself a favor and sneak a few extra games in *before* she gets a theory of mind.

Before your child is able to see another person's perspective, her hiding technique will be hilarious—she'll hole up behind the curtains twenty-seven times in a row, she'll reveal her location by giggling or shouting "You can't find me!" as soon as you get up to look, and she'll even do that adorable thing where she sits right out in the middle of the room with her eyes closed, assuming you can't see her because she can't see you.

But as soon as your kid learns to put herself in your shoes, she's going to get waaaaay better at this game. Which means her cutest hiding spots will be a thing of the past. And you'll have to actually work to find her!

It's the Thought That Counts

If you've ever flown anywhere with your child, you've been told that when those oxygen masks terrifyingly drop out of the ceiling for some reason, you're supposed to put your own mask on first, *before* helping your kid with his.

Well even though the pint-sized passenger next to you can't be trusted to go five minutes without performing an Irish step dance all over the seatback tray table in front of him, he'd probably be a real ace at following a rule like that one.

Try this simple little shopping experiment with your child to see just how important it is for him to help himself—before helping others.

Age	Ability Tested
2½–4 years	Social Development

What You Need

☛   a computer

☛   the Internet

☛   some basic online shopping skills

How It Works

☛ **PART 1**

1. Visit an online store that sells items for both kids and adults. Think Amazon or Target, not Toys "R" Us or Office Depot.

2. Put four grown-up books (or some other adult-appropriate gift) and four teddy bears (or some other child-appropriate gift) of various colors and styles into your online shopping cart. Make sure you can view all eight items on a single page.

3. Pick an adult who your child is very familiar with—like his grandmother, for example—and say to him, "We need to pick a present for Nana. Can you help me?"

4. Assuming your kid loves his grandma as much as our kids love theirs, he'll probably be totally excited to help. But before you pull up the shopping cart, prepare your child by saying, "I'm going to show you some books with lots of words and no pictures that adults like to read and some teddy bear toys. You get to pick *one thing* to give to Nana as a gift."

5. Show your child the online shopping cart, pointing out the various books and teddy bears. Ask, "Which gift would you like to give to Nana?"

6. See what gift he chooses.

☞ PART 2

1. Using the same online shopping cart stocked with four grown-up books and four teddy bears, choose another adult who your child knows well and would love to buy a gift for—like Grandpa.

2. This time tell your child, "Now I need you to help me pick *two* gifts. One of the gifts is going to be for *you*! The other gift is going to be for Grandpa. I'm going to show you books with lots of words and no pictures that adults like to read and some teddy bear toys. You get to pick one gift for you and then one gift for Grandpa."

3. Show your child the online shopping cart and ask, "Which gift would you like for you?"

4. See which gift he chooses for himself. (And don't worry—if your kid's anything like ours, he will soon forget about the toy and you'll be off the hook for actually buying it.)

5. Now ask your child, "Which gift would you like for Grandpa?"

6. See which gift he chooses for the adult this time.

If *you* had to figure out which gift to get Grandpa, it would be easy, right? You'd obviously pick out one of the four grown-up books in your shopping cart—*plus* a superexciting gift certificate to Office Depot. (Go crazy, Grandpa!)

But your three- or four-year-old child probably had a much harder time selecting an age-appropriate gift during this experiment—especially during Part 1. When you told your kid he could only pick one gift out of the cart, he probably chose to give the adult the teddy bear toy that he really wanted for himself. (And if he reacted like our daughter when we did this test with her, he made his decision *immediately* and with full-bodied enthusiasm.) During Part 2 on the other hand, chances are good he chose the teddy bear for himself first but then chose one of the grown-up books for the adult.

In both parts of the experiment, your kid was tasked with choosing an adult-appropriate gift. But when he wasn't given the option to pick a gift for himself also, he became paralyzed by his own desire. He wanted that bear. He *needed* that bear. And if he couldn't have that bear, by golly his *Nana* was going to get that bear! Only after you satisfied his overwhelming need to get his greedy little hands all over one of those amazing-looking bears was your shopaholic shorty able to think clearly enough to consider somebody else's feelings.

It's not that kids don't know which gifts are right for their grandparents. In fact, the researchers who created this study had children first sort a collection of objects (like a purse, lipstick, cookbook, doll, bottle, and toy truck) into two separate bins depending on whether they belonged to adults or kids before they even started the gift-giving task. They found that although kids had no problem identifying who the objects were for, they still couldn't pick an appropriate gift for an adult until they had gotten their own gift (or the promise of a gift) first. Satisfying their own desires first freed up kids to think about another person. Before that, they simply couldn't do it.

Gift-giving is a hard task even for adults—and many of us are probably much worse at it than we think. Research shows that adults, just like children, are more influenced by their personal preferences than they realize. For example, researchers once asked adults whether they preferred music from the 1960s or the 1980s. Then they asked the same adults to estimate what percentage of the population would agree with them. No matter which decade they chose, the adults in the study consistently assumed that their selection was more popular, and they overestimated the number of people who shared that opinion. So maybe when you were sure you had picked out that fabulous bottle of lavender-scented bubble bath because it was "just perfect for Pop Pop," you actually selected it because you were secretly fantasizing about some much-needed pampering for yourself.

This experiment is really hard because not only do kids have to consider someone else's point of view, they also have to fulfill that person's desires when they are in direct conflict with their own. Some three-year-olds *still* can't pick the adult-appropriate gift even after they have gotten a gift first. The task of controlling their own overpowering desires is just too demanding on their still-developing brains.

And do you know what makes this test even harder? Research suggests that self-control is a limited commodity, even in adults. As parents, we use self-control to prevent ourselves from going back to sleep after a child has woken us up at 6:00 AM, to keep from screaming at our kids in response to a frustrating tantrum, and to remind ourselves that happy hour really isn't supposed to start until the late afternoon. But because self-control is a limited resource, each time we use some we deplete our stash a little, which makes it that much harder to summon the strength to use it again later. No wonder parenting is so exhausting!

And if using self-control is a difficult exercise for *us* throughout the day, imagine how hard it must be for our kids. Keeping this in mind may help you to be more understanding of your child's limitations, to avoid placing too many demands on him, and maybe even to better exercise your own self-control when it's tested by the limits of your child's.

Tips to Help Your Child

One thing we really like about this experiment is how empowering it is for your child. By turning over control of your online shopping cart to your kid, you're allowing him to help you make a decision (even if it is a totally fake decision that you're never actually going to follow through with). Giving your child choices throughout the day can be a fun way to help build his sense of independence and avoid behavior issues.

Because young kids have very little actual power in their lives, giving them license to make some choices—even if they're prescribed, preapproved, not-actually-independent choices—can make them feel autonomous and in control of *something*. So try letting him pick the shirt he wears, what he eats for lunch from a couple of options you've already narrowed down, or which presidential candidate you'll vote for.

You know, the little things.

Tips to Help Yourself

In this experiment, your child was paralyzed by his irresistible longing for a new toy. If you spend *any* time with a preschooler, you know this is a typical part of almost any day. Your child is constantly seeing cool new toys, books, lunchboxes, and slightly different colored versions of all sorts of things he already owns, which he just absolutely *cannot live without*. This can be debilitating for both him and you, as it can lead to constant requests, tearful pleas, and even full-blown fits.

Luckily, we've put together a totally effective trick for dealing with our children's incessant appetite for new stuff. It's saved our household lots of headaches, and may be able to do the same for yours.

Are you ready for it? Here goes:

We keep an imaginary wish list of everything our kids want. And let us tell you, this list is *massive*. Absolutely anything the kids want can go on it. We never have to write anything down since the list is imaginary, and we make our kids happy by satisfying their desires at least a little bit by implying that since something is on the list, they'll get it some day (even if they actually won't).

The list began as a birthday wish list when our daughter was asking for lots of things just before she turned two. After her birthday passed, we said the things she wanted could go on a Christmas list. After that it was a Valentine's Day list—and Valentine's Day lists *don't even exist*.

Eventually the birthdays and holidays just disappeared, and things she wanted just went on "her list." Now whenever she asks if she can have something, we say, "That looks like a great thing to put on your list!" She's happy because she's been heard, and we're happy because we didn't have to hear her over and over and over.

The list is so effective that the other day we were able to draw our daughter out of the toy section at the store by telling her that we were putting *all* the toys in the store on her list.

Sometimes you just stumble upon parenting magic. And it feels *awesome.*

Mini Memorizer

Waaaay back before you had kids (or any real responsibilities whatsoever), you may remember attending a party or two where everybody drank cheap booze out of even cheaper red plastic cups. Of course, depending on how many times you filled/emptied your cup, you may *not* remember those parties much at all.

This experiment flips the way you've used those classic cups right on its head. Instead of causing *your* memory to get fuzzier, they can now help *your kid's* memory get sharper than ever.

Age	Ability Tested
3–4 years	Memory

What You Need

- ☛ 8 identical opaque cups (Since you're not throwing any raging kegger parties anytime soon, those red plastic ones collecting dust in the pantry will be perfect.)

- ☛ 2 toy animals small enough to be hidden underneath any of those overturned cups

- ☛ a table and two chairs

- ☛ a video camera, video baby monitor, or adult accomplice to help you discreetly watch your child's behavior during the experiment—optional, but recommended

How It Works

1. Place the eight cups upside down on a table, forming a semi-circle right in front of the chair where your child will be sitting. Have one toy animal (let's say it's a dog) with you at the table and the second toy animal stashed out of sight in a nearby room—preferably one that has a clear view of the table, cups, and chairs.

2. Using the toy dog and cups as props, tell your child a story. Start by saying, "I want to tell you a story about this dog," and show her the toy dog.

3. As you say, "Here he is on the playground. He loves to play. He runs. He jumps," pantomime the toy dog running around on the table and playing in front of the semicircle of cups.

4. Continue the story by saying, "But he was playing so much that he got very hungry. So he went to look for some food. When he was looking for food, he went by *this* dog house, and *this* dog house, and *this* dog house, and *this* dog house, and *this* dog house." As you refer to each "dog house," walk your toy dog past one of the cups. Start on one end of the semicircle and walk him past five cups or so in this way.

5. Say, "And then he went in *this* dog house to find some food." Lift up the next cup and place the dog underneath it.

6. Abruptly pause the story by saying, "You know what? I have another toy I could get to help us tell the story. I'll go get it. While I go get it, you *remember* where the dog is. I'll be right back. You *remember* where the dog is."

7. Now pay attention, because this is the important part of the experiment. Leave your child at the table for about one minute

while you retrieve the other toy animal you've stashed. But what's most important here is that you secretly pay attention to what your child is doing now that the game is paused. Notice things like what she looks at, what she touches, and how she occupies her time. Since this is the most important part of the experiment, you may want to videotape it or have another adult covertly watch your child so you can further analyze (or just be entertained by) your kid's behavior.

8. After about a minute, return and ask your child, "Now, where is the dog? You find the dog so I can tell you the rest of the story."

9. After your kid shows you where the dog is, finish up by completing the story. It can be quick ("Then the dog and the other animal jumped around together. The end.") or elaborate ("The dog met the other animal, and they decided to go into business together, buying up all of these dog houses on the cheap, then installing travertine floors and granite countertops so they could flip them for a huge profit. But first they had to incorporate their new company in Nevada for tax purposes, then spend several weeks deciding on the perfect font for their company letterhead."). It really doesn't matter how you end it—the experiment is over at this point, so now you're just playing!

What did your child do for the minute you were gone? Did she just sit there passively waiting for you to return? Or did she show signs that she was actively trying to remember where the toy was? In this situation, kids often do the latter. They try things like looking at, pointing at, or touching the cup with the dog under it. They may even peek under the cup as if to reinforce their belief that yes, the hound is hiding right there!

These purposeful strategies for remembering the toy's location are noteworthy because they represent children's earliest attempts at actively trying to commit something to memory. As adults, when we try to remember something, we have lots of really effective and practiced strategies for doing it: we can synthesize information into a more easily remembered form (like "third cup from the left"), repeat the information over and over in our minds, or create a mental picture, story, or acronym related to the information we need to retain. Kids don't typically start using any of these more sophisticated memory strategies until they're at least five or six years old. But the roots of such strategies can be seen in your kid's concerted attempts to remember in this task.

And these conscious efforts to remember actually do pay off. The researchers who created this experiment asked a group of kids to remember the location of the dog while they went away for a minute (just as you did in this experiment), but did *not* ask another group of kids to remember in the same situation. For those kids, the experimenter simply walked away for a minute to go grab another toy. The results of the experiment showed that kids who were asked to remember used a lot more of these memory strategies (looking, pointing, touching, and peeking)—and they were also a lot better at remembering where the toy was as a result.

Even though your preschooler has probably never even heard of a pop quiz yet, she's already a quick study. By watching her apply her creative and clever mind to solving problems like this one, you can see the beginnings of the future student she'll be someday. And that day is coming sooner than you can ever imagine. So remember to treat every moment you have with your little one like a pooch under a plastic cup— stare at it as long as you can so you'll never, ever forget it.

Tips to Help Your Child

One powerful way to help boost kids' memories is to make the thing they're trying to remember *meaningful* to them. One research study tested this idea by asking two different groups of kids to remember a list of groceries. In one group, children were told to remember the food items so they could tell the list to another person. In the other group, children were told to remember the items so they could get them at a store and use them to make a sack lunch to share with a parent. Kids who heard about the meaningful lunch activity remembered significantly more food items than those who were simply asked to remember.

It's not just kids who benefit by making information more meaningful. At any age, people remember information better when it is processed more deeply. The more you think about new information and relate it to previous knowledge, the more easily you will recall it later. So a good strategy for anyone who wants to remember something is to integrate the new knowledge into what they already know by trying to generate personally relevant examples.

Your child is too young to start using this memory trick on her own, but you can help do it for her. When teaching her about a new topic, help her understand and remember it by relating it to things she already knows. For example, when explaining how trees take in water and minerals from the soil to help them grow, you can liken it to the way people and animals eat food and drink water. And by adding in the even more personal example of how she helps Daddy feed the family cat, you can really make it meaningful to her.

Tips to Help Yourself

Did you know you could use your child's budding ability to purposefully remember to your advantage? In one study, an experimenter took children ages three to five for a walk, during which the experimenter dropped her keys. Kids who were *asked* to remember the location of the keys were much better at finding them later.

When we first came across this study, it gave us a great idea. We could just start asking our preschooler to remember stuff for us throughout the day:

"Oh, I put my keys on the piano. Can you help me remember?"

"Please try to help Mommy remember that we need milk from the store."

"Remember that we parked on the Blue level, row G, space number 4758, will you?"

OK, OK. So maybe tasking our three-year-old with being our full-time personal assistant isn't the best idea we ever had. But keep in mind your child's growing ability to remember, because she's becoming one deft little helper. And chances are she would be happy to lend an occasional hand when something really important does come up. Even if your kid doesn't end up remembering whatever it was you told her, the fact that you said it out loud in the first place might help *you* remember on your own.

The Young Switcheroo

As a parent, you've become an expert at jumping from one thing to another. You can get the kids dressed, read them a book, change a diaper, break up a fight, wipe away some tears, and complete a super-fun tickle session—all without overcooking the scrambled eggs.

But as far as your kid is concerned, switching from one task to another is still really tough.

This experiment lets you find out just how flexible your bambino's brain currently is—and teaches you one *grande* way his results could improve.

Age	Ability Tested
3–4 years	Problem Solving

What You Need

☛ a set of special cards like the ones pictured here—using blank index cards make your own set consisting of:

✳ one black heart card

✳ one white star card

✳ five white heart cards

✳ five black star cards

- 👉 two trays or boxes to sort the cards into
- 👉 some tape
- 👉 the ability to count to ten

How It Works

👉 SETUP

1. Label the two boxes by taping the black heart card to one of them and the white star card to the other. Place the two boxes next to each other on a table, so their labels are clearly visible.

2. Shuffle the remaining five white heart and five black star cards together, placing them in a single stack face down on the table.

3. Sit at the table with your child.

👉 PART 1

1. Tell your child, "This is the color game. In the color game, the black ones go here," (*point to the box with the black heart*) "and the white ones go here" (*point to the box with the white star*).

2. Hand your child a card from the top of the stack and remind him, "Remember, the black ones go *here* and the white ones go *here*." Let him place the card face down in whichever box he chooses.

3. For only the *first* card that your child places, tell him whether he was right or wrong—"Yes, you put it in the right stack!" or "Oops, that should have gone in the other stack." Do *not* give him feedback for any future cards.

4. Hand the remaining cards in the stack to him one at a time for sorting, reminding him each time, "Remember, the white ones go *here* and the black ones go *here*."

5. Make a note of how many cards your kid places correctly.

☞ PART 2

1. Reshuffle the cards and place them in a stack on the table.

2. Tell your child, "OK, now we're going to switch and play a new game: the shape game. In the shape game, the hearts go here," (*point to the box with the black heart*) "and the stars go here" (*point to the box with the white star*).

3. Hand your child a card from the top of the stack and remind him, "Remember, the heart ones go *here* and the star ones go *here*."

4. Hand the remaining cards in the stack to him one by one for him to sort, reminding him each time, "Remember, the heart ones go *here* and the star ones go *here*."

5. Make a note of how many cards your kid places correctly this time.

You probably noticed that because of the way the rules were set up for each game, the correct card placement in Part 2 was the *opposite* of the correct card placement in Part 1. (If you didn't notice that, then, um, we're pretty sure you screwed up your kid's score.) This rule reversal means your kid would have had to completely change the way he was thinking midway through the experiment in order to ace the whole test.

But that's not what happened for you, is it? Odds are, your kid posted worse scores when he tried to do Part 2.

The problem with switching rules is *not* that younger kids can't remember the new rules. They can. If, right after your three-year-old bungled up the second half of this experiment, you asked him, "Where do the black and white ones go in the color game?" and "Where do the hearts and stars go in the shape game?" he'd be able to give you the right answers.

It's just that while performing experiments like these, young children tend to *perseverate*, or get stuck thinking about, the rules that they were initially trained on. When you told your child to concentrate on whether the object on each card was black or white, it was pretty easy for him. After all, kids have an automatic tendency to learn and follow a set of rules. But when you ask them to change their strategy and start sorting the cards according to each object's shape instead of color, that requires some pretty advanced mental maneuvering. First, they have to hold two separate sets of conflicting rules in their heads, and then they have to consciously decide to *ignore* the first set of rules they learned. And that's just too much for most three-year-olds to handle. Which is why even though you repeatedly told your kid he should be sorting by shape in Part 2, he couldn't help but continue to sort by color.

And he'll probably keep doing this until somewhere between ages four and five. At that point, he should start perseverating a lot less, acquire the ability to switch seamlessly from one set of rules to another within the same game, and have no trouble categorizing the cards—no matter which way you ask him to sort them!

Tips to Help Your Child

Want to know the single biggest thing you can do to improve your kid's performance in tasks like this?

Si? you say.

Teach him a second language, we reply.

Research shows that bilingual kids can successfully complete this game about a full year earlier than kids who *no habla* anything but their primary language. That's a really big boost, considering your child has only been on this planet for a few years total!

But the relationship between being bilingual and succeeding in this task makes sense when you consider that children who are bilingual have to continually switch between one language (or one set of rules) and another. Because bilingual people are constantly holding two sets of rules for language in their heads, their brains get lots of practice restraining one language in order to speak the other.

That means that in everyday conversations, a bilingual person's brain is working harder than a monolingual person's brain. This adds up to a lot of extra mental exercise—which pays off in better cognitive skills and brain health. In fact, it's been shown that people who speak two languages enjoy a seven- to ten-year delay in the onset of Alzheimer's disease. Although older adults are advised to exercise their brains by playing video games and doing crossword puzzles to stave off dementia, a bilingual person gets this sort of extra brain exercise just by talking!

So consider exposing your child to a second language. Although learning one can initially take a lot of time and effort, being bilingual can provide your child with lifelong (and even life-lengthening) benefits.

Tips to Help Yourself

As your little one gets bigger and bigger, you're bound to discover that some of the rules you established (or failed to establish) early on might require some tweaking down the line. And *we* know from experience that once you try to lay down the *new* law, your kids may not take too kindly to it. This whole perseveration thing can help explain why.

For example:

Perhaps you got into the habit of putting your child to bed each night and then wandering around, cleaning up all of his toys, books, peeled-off backs of stickers, previously missing socks, and half-eaten slices of apple he's left strewn all over the house. Then one day, you realize that *you* shouldn't be doing all this work, so you institute a new rule that *he* needs to pick up before bedtime. Crying, whining, and lots of "I'm too tired"s are sure to follow. The same thing could happen if you always let him run around and play during dinner, and then go out to eat, expecting him to magically sit down and behave just because you're at a restaurant.

Even the dimwitted busboy who keeps trying to clear your plate when you're obviously still nibbling at your flourless molten lava chocolate torte could've told you that just wasn't gonna happen.

The tough-to-swallow truth is that you successfully taught your child some rules (that he never has to pick up his toys and never has to sit down at mealtime), and trying to get his perseverating little brain to ignore them in favor of a whole new set of rules now is next to impossible.

So what can you do to fix this situation? Not a lot, unfortunately. Be consistent and stand behind your new rules even if it's hard—because flip-flopping will only teach your kid that fighting you on an issue may be a good way to get you to change your mind. Then just ride it out the best you can until he turns five, when his mental flexibility ought to improve.

In the meantime, you can definitely use the lessons learned here to help you with any *new* rules that come up. Like when it's time to upgrade your phone, you can institute the rule that *this* phone is for Mommy and Daddy *only*. Spell out your position right away before there's time to pick up any bad habits—and don't back down from it, even if your little cutie really, *really* needs to take a selfie right now.

For Realsies

Your pipsqueak probably *loves* pretending. This closet? It's her house. That teddy bear? It's her baby. The cat? It's her horse. And her riding lesson is about to start!

(Sorry about that, Kitty.)

Although your child knows what pretend play is—and she's doing more and more of it every day—this experiment shows that there are *some* things she still has to learn about fantasy versus reality.

Age	Ability Tested
3–5 years	Social Development

What You Need
- ☞ you
- ☞ your child
- ☞ at least some small inkling of what cartoons your kid likes to watch

How It Works

This experiment consists of a simple set of questions for both you and your kid to answer. Before you start, think of two sets of characters from two different cartoons you and your child are both familiar with. Here are some potential examples (although you can use any two sets of characters that you both know well):

* Mickey Mouse, Donald Duck, and Goofy

* Papa Smurf, Brainy Smurf, and Smurfette

* Buttershy, Twilight Sparkle, and Applejack

* Speedy Cerviche, Meowzma O' Tool, and Big Al Dente (although if these guys make your list, your kid has a truly unusual appreciation for weird, vintage Japanese anime)

☛ PART 1

After you've selected your two sets of characters, think about your answers for each question below one at a time, without reading ahead. We used the first two sets of characters in this example, so just substitute the names of whichever characters you chose as needed.

1. Think about the characters from each of the cartoons you chose:

   * Do you think Mickey Mouse is real or pretend? Is Donald Duck real or pretend? How about Goofy?

   * Do you think Papa Smurf is real or pretend? Is Smurfette real or pretend? How about Brainy Smurf?

2. Think about how a character from *one* cartoon would view a character from the *other* cartoon (and vice-versa):

    ✳ Does Donald Duck think that Papa Smurf is real or pretend?

    ✳ Does Smurfette think that Mickey Mouse is real or pretend?

3. Think about how characters from each cartoon would view other characters in their *own* cartoon:

    ✳ Does Mickey Mouse think that Goofy is real or pretend?

    ✳ Does Papa Smurf think that Brainy Smurf is real or pretend?

Figured out all your answers? Good! Let's see how they match up to everybody else's. The researchers who originated this study found that on average, adults tend to respond to these questions in the following ways:

* For Question 1, just about all adults agree cartoon characters are *pretend*. Nothing too shocking there.

* For Question 2, the majority of adults feel characters in one cartoon would think characters in a different cartoon are *pretend*. (Although, the authors of this book would argue it's perfectly logical to believe that all 'toons could coexist in some collective fantasy world where they all see each other as real. But since this question isn't actually that important to this experiment, we're willing to let it slide.)

* For Question 3, we're back to being pretty straightforward again, as most adults say characters would believe other characters in their own cartoon are *real*.

How It Works

☛ PART 2

Ask your child all the same questions you've already answered yourself—then compare your answers. Are they all the same? If not, what's different?

Based on how most children between the ages of three and six answer these questions, we're pretty sure your kid's responses went something like this:

* Pretend.

* Pretend.

* Pretend.

For the first two sets of questions, that's not surprising—and it's most likely how you answered them too. But for Question 3, your child's answer almost certainly differed from yours. The original researchers who developed this study found that although almost all adults agree characters in the same cartoon would see each other as *real*, almost all young kids agree characters in the same cartoon would see each other as *pretend*.

This is pretty crazy, right? How can you live in the same mushroom village as a bunch of people who eat the same smurfberries as you, run away from the same evil, cat-loving wizard as you, and look just like you (all the way down to the white cap, blue skin, and three-apple height) and *not* think that they're real? As Donald Duck might say, what's the big idea here?

Well it's actually pretty simple. You've already seen your child demonstrate that she has a hard time taking on another person's perspective in both the "Think Inside the Box" and "It's the Thought That Counts" experiments earlier in this book. A three- or four-year-old child is not yet capable of putting herself in the mind of another human being to imagine what that person might be thinking. And she probably won't be until about age five. Because this particular experiment involves the added difficulty of trying to get inside the head of someone who is not even the same species as her *and* not even real, it could very well take even longer to master.

Or maybe not—if you just give your child a little help shifting her point of view.

The original researchers repeated this study, except before asking kids about whether characters thought other characters in the same cartoon were real or pretend, they first asked kids about whether these characters could see, touch, and talk to each other. "Can Smurfette see Papa Smurf?" "Can Smurfette touch Papa Smurf?" "Can Smurfette talk to Papa Smurf?" After kids heard these questions that forced them to really think about someone else's perspective, they were much more likely to say those characters thought the others were real!

Tips to Help Your Child

During the preschool years, pretend play tends to develop from an activity kids do by themselves to one that is shared and collectively constructed with peers. Creating pretend scenarios with other kids is a complex practice that requires communicating, negotiating control, and building a story. And if you want to help your child build these skills, you can—simply by playing *with* her!

Because you have so much more play experience, as well as a considerably more advanced understanding of other people's thoughts and feelings, you can serve as the perfect role model to help your child create more elaborate pretend play scenarios and channel her creativity into more coherent stories. For example, your kid would probably be perfectly happy simply putting play food on plates and handing you new dishes she's "cooked" for you all day long. But if you become an active participant in her playtime, you can elevate that basic activity into something much more complex—the two of you could be running your own restaurant, which needs a name and a menu, plus pads of paper and pens so you can take customers' orders, and if you can cook the perfect meal for the important food critic that's coming in tonight, maybe you can get that Michelin star you've been coveting your entire career, which will let you raise your prices through the roof and finally land your picture on the cover of *Overpriced Hors d'Oeuvres* magazine!

Even if you take it a little too far (like that restaurant thing may have done), watching you interact in high-level ways with your imagined scenarios will help your budding storyteller build the skills she needs to more effectively pretend with peers.

But when playing with your child, remember to share the lead. Try to observe how she is playing, and enter under pretenses she has already created. Resist the urge to take over and control the play—you'll both get more out of it that way.

Tips to Help Yourself

Your personal development doesn't have to stop just because you're an adult. Research shows that grown-ups who read more fiction tend to be better at reading facial expressions and understanding the emotions of others. And you want to know one of the genres that can give your empathy the biggest boost? Romance novels.

So the next time you're at a library or airport bookstore, don't feel bad about picking up some of the sleaziest titles you find. They'll totally help you set a good reading example for your child, develop your own empathy skills—and get some cheap thrills while you're at it!

I Am Not an Animal!

Your kid climbs like a monkey, leaps like a frog, looks cute as a bug, and makes messes like a pig. But at the end of the day, he's the most amazing little human being you've ever seen.

Although it's easy for you to appreciate the many different sides of your child all at once, thinking about something in multiple ways at the same time is quite a bit tougher for your child. Perform this experiment on your cuddly little snuggle bunny, and you'll see exactly what we mean.

Age	Abilities Tested
3–7 years	Problem Solving, Categorization, Math

What You Need

- ☞ 5 or 6 small toys that are all one type of animal (like dogs)

- ☞ 2 small toys that are *another* type of animal (like cows)

- ☞ You don't actually need this for the experiment, but wouldn't it be great if you had some sort of magical, Dr. Seussian, small-toy-vacuuming-and-sorting machine that could suck up and spit out into organized containers all the dogs, cows, and other tiny plastic knick-knacks your kid dumps out and scatters all over the house over and over, every freaking day?

- ☞ Seriously, wouldn't that be awesome?

How It Works

1. Stand up all of the toys together on a flat surface.

2. Naming whichever animal you have the *most* of, ask your child, "Are there more *dogs* or more *animals*?"

3. See what *your* little animal says.

Ha! Did your kiddo fall for this trick, or what?

You asked if there were more dogs or more animals. Since dogs *are* animals, and you put out some dogs *and* some cows—which the last time we checked, just so happen to be animals too—then obviously *animals* is the right answer.

But your kid probably didn't see it this way.

It's as if your child heard the question you asked him, and then mentally revised it to be "Are there more dogs or more *other* animals?" Even if you ask the question repeatedly, your child will probably persist in saying there are more dogs. After we did this experiment on our daughter, we asked her, "How do you know?" She responded, "Because there are lots of dogs." (The *Duh*, Mom and Dad" part was only strongly implied.)

That's what's particularly funny about this experiment. Kids between three and seven years old will be excited to take part in the test because by this point, they've become regular whizzes at counting. So when you pose a question that seems to be simply about adding up some animals, they think it's really easy—and are happy to immediately give you the obvious answer. The only problem with that? Their answer is completely wrong.

This experiment was created by a wildly famous, well-respected, and insightful pioneer in the study of child development, Jean Piaget. He knew this experiment was not just a children's riddle but rather a test of a child's ability to simultaneously weigh multiple aspects of a situation to solve a problem. The reason young children answer this question incorrectly is that they immediately recognize the dog toys should be classified as "dogs," but they fail to realize they should *also* be classified as "animals."

According to Piaget, developing the ability to correctly answer questions like this one is a major milestone in children's cognitive development. Once kids can do it, it's a sign they have become much more creative and critical thinkers, capable of applying their newfound skills to tackle all sorts of problems, both in and out of the classroom.

Tips to Help Your Child

Because your child was fooled by this experiment, you might be tempted to think he doesn't understand much about numbers. You wouldn't be alone. Even a brilliant theorist like Piaget believed children were hopeless with numbers until they were about seven years old. But you (like Piaget) would be wrong to underestimate children's thinking this way.

Despite their difficulty with problems like this one, young kids are actually capable of understanding many basic math concepts even before they start kindergarten. Preschool-aged children can count, identify the relative sizes of numbers (like six is bigger than four), and do simple addition and subtraction.

Developing number skills like these before kindergarten is actually really important, because children's relative understanding of numbers in kindergarten is highly predictive of their later math achievement. The better children are at these basic number concepts early on, the better their math grades will be through high school.

But don't panic just because your kid hasn't memorized a whole bunch of times tables yet. We're not suggesting you put your child through intensive math drills, lengthy number-flashcard sessions, or high-priced private tutoring. Rather, you can easily help develop these important number skills through simple, everyday interactions: counting the stairs together as you walk up or down, doing simple addition and subtraction problems with grapes at snack time, and playing card and board games that involve numbers.

Just a little number experience goes a long way. One study showed that playing number line games in which game pieces move along numbered spaces (like Chutes and Ladders) for just four sessions of fifteen minutes each gave preschool-aged children measurable gains in number skills. And these gains persisted for several weeks after this limited play.

And while you're working on integrating more number talk and play into your daily routine, be sure to provide *equal-opportunity* number experience. Research shows that American parents are twice as likely to talk to boys about numbers than girls. So it's cool if you want to raise a little princess—but do her a favor and make sure she knows how to count all the jewels in her tiara!

Tips to Help Yourself

If you ever find yourself at a social gathering mingling with a bunch of developmental psychologists, just name-drop Piaget (pronounced PEE-a-jhay), and they'll automatically treat you like you're the life of the party. Any of the following off-the-cuff remarks ought to work:

* "Who does that guy think he is, Piaget?"
* "It's like these people have never heard of Piaget or something!"
* "Piaget, am I right?"
* "To Piaget!"

Then clink your glasses, give a bunch of enthusiastic high fives, and wait for the Facebook friend requests to start pouring in.

Pants on Fire

You know the story about how when George Washington was six years old, he nobly admitted to chopping down his dad's favorite cherry tree by saying, "I cannot tell a lie"?

People always use this as an example of how virtuous and honest our first president was. But you know what? It could be that he just wasn't old enough to be any good at lying yet. If he'd waited a couple of years before deciding to become an axe-wielding maniac, he very well might've blamed his brother.

This fun little experiment allows you to track the development of *your* kid's lying abilities—so you can determine exactly when you become totally screwed.

Age	Ability Tested
3–7 years	Social Development

What You Need

☞ a basket full of a bunch of noise-making toys, plus one toy that doesn't make noise

☞ a blanket or bath towel

☞ a table and two chairs

☞ a video camera or video baby monitor for covertly viewing your child's behavior (optional but recommended, especially for your own entertainment value)

☞ a prize

How It Works

☞ SETUP

1. Fill a basket with several of your child's noisiest toys—talking dolls, musical instruments, toy phones, cymbal-playing monkeys, and the like. Shoot for at least six toys that make as specific and unique noises as possible.

2. Add one toy to your basket that does *not* make noise—like a soccer ball, block, or stuffed animal. Cover the basket and all its contents with a blanket or bath towel.

3. Set up your table with the two chairs across from one another. One chair (where you'll be sitting) should be facing *toward* the table, and the other chair (where your child will be sitting)

should be facing *away* from the table, so that when she sits down she'll be completely unable to see you or the table.

4. Place the basket of toys, covered by the bath towel, next to your chair.

5. If possible, set up a video camera or video baby monitor to capture what your child does during the experiment.

☛ THE EXPERIMENT

1. Ask your child to play a guessing game with you, telling her, "Each time I play a noise from one of your toys, you have to guess which toy it is without looking. If you can guess three right, you'll get a prize!"

2. Sit down at the table with your child. Even though her back will be facing you, you should still remind her not to peek each time you take out a toy.

3. Pull one toy from your basket, place it on the table, and play its noise—then let your child guess which toy it is. Repeat with the other toys until she correctly guesses two toys.

4. Now that your kid is only one correct guess away from winning her prize, take out the toy that does *not* make noise, place it on the table, and snap your fingers a few times.

5. Immediately (before your child has a chance to guess what this new toy is) say you have to leave the room for a minute, but that you'll be right back. Before you leave, tell your child, "Remember not to peek. I am going to leave this toy on the table, and when I get back you can have your prize if you guess it correctly. Remember, no peeking!"

6. Leave the room for about a minute. If you've got a baby monitor set up, watch it now.

7. Walk back to the room, giving your child advance warning that you're coming by singing or talking loudly. As soon as you get back, cover the toy with the towel.

8. Ask your child, "So what do you think the toy is?"

9. If she answers correctly, ask her, "How did you know? Did you peek while I was gone?" (If she doesn't answer, assure her you won't be mad no matter what she says.) If your kid answers incorrectly, pull out new toys and play their sounds until she gets her third guess right.

10. Give your little guesser the prize!

So did your kid guess the noiseless toy correctly? If so, congratulations! You can officially not trust another word that ever comes out of her mouth! Clearly there was no way for her to know what this item was based on the sound it made (because it didn't make one), so if she guessed it right, she almost certainly peeked. And if she told you she *didn't* peek, then she just lied, too.

This experiment mimics one of the earliest types of lies children learn to tell—denying doing something an adult has told them not to do. If it makes you feel any better about what your own child just did to you, please know that most children peek in this experiment, and most children also lie about it. But not *all* kids do. Of the three-year-olds who do peek, for instance, about half actually admit they've done so when asked—presumably because they have not yet started to develop skills in lying.

So enjoy that while it lasts, will ya?

Even when the fibs do start flying, it should be fairly easy for you to tell—at least for the first few years. Research shows that children younger than eight aren't that great at lying yet. In one study, adults observing children answer follow-up questions from an experiment like this one were able to accurately guess whether the kids were lying—even though they didn't know any of the children personally or whether the children had peeked or not. So without much prodding at all, most kids (especially the younger ones) are going to give themselves away.

On the other hand, some kids are such savvy liars that they peek but then actually guess a *different* toy than the one that they know it to be, just so they can throw you off track. Increasingly sophisticated forms of trickery like this get more common with age. So once your kid hits six or seven, watch out. You might want to start sleeping with one eye open. And your wallet wedged between your thighs.

When our daughter was three, she started experimenting with lies. On one occasion, we gave her a cookie to eat while she was with a baby-sitter, and after we returned we asked her if she enjoyed the treat. She responded, "Oh, I think Freddy ate my cookie." We were surprised. The cookie was pretty big for her one-year-old brother to have eaten—and frankly neither one of us could imagine a situation where she would even let that guy *near* her special dessert. We were baffled. Furrowed brows, tongues hanging out—the works. But then she decided to clarify her answer, saying, "Oh, I mean it fell on the floor and got dirty so no one could eat it." At that point we realized our little girl was trying to dupe us into letting her have a second cookie. We asked her if she was lying, and she responded, "I'm not lying. I'm just joking!"

Our daughter's confusion was understandable, considering that both lies and jokes often involve intentionally saying or doing something you know is false. But understanding a lie requires a more complex knowledge of another person's intentions, because it necessitates knowing not only that someone has said something untrue but also that it has been said to intentionally trick another person. That's why children typically learn to understand jokes before they understand lies.

As irksome as it can be to us parents, lying actually represents pretty smart thinking. To lie to you effectively, your child has to get inside your head and accurately assess what you do and do not know. She also has to plan a plausible cover story, hold a lot of conflicting information in her memory (like what actually happened versus the fake story she's concocted), and control herself so she doesn't accidentally spill the beans. That's a lot for a young brain to take on all at once.

It's also why a child's lying ability is related to her overall intelligence.

Kids who lie in situations like this study tend to score higher in tests of planning, problem solving, and the ability to selectively pay attention to information—which are all important aspects of general intelligence. So if this experiment revealed you've got a little liar in the making, at least it means she's probably pretty brainy, too!

Tips to Help Your Child

Want to help your kid get *better* at lying? Of course you don't (unless you're a total masochist). That's why it's important to watch your *own* behavior, so you can avoid entrapping your child into telling more lies than she needs to.

A major reason kids lie is to avoid punishment, so if you already know your child has done something wrong, asking her if she's done it will only invite her to lie to you about it. For example, if you walk into the kitchen where your child is eating lunch and find food all over the floor, you have a pretty good idea who made the mess. Yet for some reason, your first instinct is probably to ask (in a very angry voice), "Did *you* throw this food all over the floor?" Your child doesn't want to disappoint you—and doubly doesn't want to be punished—so if you ask her whether she did it, a lie may be too tempting to resist.

Instead of a question, try going straight to a statement. "I see that you threw your food on the floor. That makes me very upset, because it is *not* the way we treat our food. Now you're going to need to clean this mess up." You can still say all this in an angry voice if it makes you feel better.

Forcing your child into unnecessary lies can actually lead to *more* lying in the long run. Although all kids practice some amount of lying, research shows that as lying becomes more prevalent, it can lead to more serious delinquent behavior in the future. Practice with lying makes perfect, and the difference between today's minor offenses and the world-rocking doozies that tomorrow might bring is only a matter of degrees.

Tips to Help Yourself

Now that your little con artist is getting a taste for untruths, you're going to want to arm yourself with as many lie-detecting tricks as possible. Here are some common indications that your child may be trying to pull the wool over your eyes:

* *Verbal leakage.* Like you saw in this experiment, it's common for your child to inadvertently reveal her lies in her speech. So ask for more detail, and she might leak clues about whether or not she's telling the truth.

* *Improbable details.* Children's false stories are more likely to contain more fantastical or improbable details than their true ones. For example, the gerbil almost certainly did *not* eat your kid's report card.

* *More new information on retelling.* When children tell true stories repeatedly, they are more likely to include the same information over and over and are less likely to add new information. But because made-up stories are not constrained by the facts of actual events, children's lies often change more over time.

* *Big smiles.* Children who are lying are more likely to be flashing their pearly whites like a politician, while children who do not lie tend to have relaxed expressions. So even though they are completely adorable, be extra leery of your child's wide smiles whenever you suspect foul play.

Doodle-y Noted

Whether you're listening to an automated voice tell you the next available customer service representative will "be with you shortly," cramming your body into an entirely too tiny desk while waiting for your parent-teacher conference to begin, or watching your child's favorite mind-numbingly moronic TV show for what seems like the two hundredth time this week, everybody zones out from time to time.

And when that happens, you'll sometimes find yourself scribbling little designs, drawings, and doodles all over whatever piece of paper (or exposed section of skin) happens to be in front of you.

But for your kid, doodling can do way more than just pass the time. Perform this easily repeatable experiment-disguised-as-a-game with your child to see how sophisticated his little memory is getting—plus end up with an adorable keepsake from the experience too!

Age	Abilities Tested
3 years and older	Memory, Symbol Use

What You Need
- ☛ a standard Memory game featuring pairs of cards with matching pictures on them
- ☛ some paper
- ☛ your kid's favorite writing instrument

How It Works

1. Set up the memory game like you normally would, shuffling the cards and laying them out in rows.

2. Before you start the game, give your kid some paper and something to write with, and tell him he can use them to write down *whatever he wants* to help him during the game. Pictures, words, lyrics to his favorite 1960s war protest anthem—anything he thinks will help him remember the location of the cards so he can find matches more easily.

3. Play the game like usual, taking turns flipping over cards to look for matches.

4. Pay special attention to how your kid chooses to use his notes.

Playing memory games with your kid is a pretty brain-friendly activity to begin with. But when you add a pencil and paper to the mix, you can learn even more about how your little one thinks.

After the game is over, take a gander at what your youngster scribbled down. Since this experiment is good for kids covering a pretty wide age range, his notes could look like almost anything. "Good" notes—those which would actually help gameplay performance—require that kids use *symbols* that are truly useful in helping them remember card locations. For example, you might draw a grid that resembles the layout of the cards, then write notes on that grid for each card you see. For the card with the flower on it, for instance, you would draw a picture that looks like a flower, or maybe just the letter *F* (which of course would *not* help you if the flower card was right next to the Fabio one).

At first, young kids will be hopeless at this. Their notes will probably look like random drawings that have nothing to do with the game. Your younger child may even become so interested in the activity of drawing that he forgets about playing the game altogether.

But as kids get older, the connection between their notes and the game will become increasingly more obvious, and their notes will become much more useful in helping them win. Researchers who did this study found that children made tremendous strides in their ability to construct helpful notes between the first and seventh grades, so look for bigger changes to happen in those years.

Interestingly, older kids eventually get so good at using notes that they actually rely on them to relieve some of the memory load needed to excel at this game. If you take away an older child's notes in the middle of the game, he'll be hopeless at remembering where matches are because he's been so effectively using the notes to tell him. Kind of like how *you'd* be completely incapable of calling your own mother if you didn't have your phone to remember her number for you.

Do this activity repeatedly over the next several years to observe how your child's skills in memory and symbol use develop. You can even keep all his old notes to do a cool side-by-side comparison!

Unless, of course, you forget to. In which case, you really ought to write yourself a note next time.

Tips to Help Your Child

Want to know an easy way to help your child learn to take good notes? Encourage him to work on his handwriting. We know, we know. That sounds totally superficial, like saying you can make somebody really love a birthday present just by putting a big, beautiful bow on it. But that's not what we're saying at all. For good penmanship to lead to effective notes, it isn't important that your child's handwriting is *pretty*—it's just important that it's *fast*.

Research shows that better note-takers are faster writers. To assess speed and fluency of writing, researchers timed students for thirty seconds while they wrote the alphabet as many times as they could. They then compared students' handwriting speed to the quality of their notes and found that those who could write more in less time also had notes that were better focused around more relevant main ideas. Being able to write faster means the process has become automatic and less mental energy is required for the task of writing itself. So fast writers can spend more energy on other things, like focusing on the lesson and organizing information to make more useful notes. And this pays off big time in the form of higher test scores.

Being able to write more quickly is also related to the ability to write better stories and essays. Research shows that children who can write more in less time tend to be rated higher on multiple measures of writing quality. Just as being able to write quickly and automatically frees learners up to take good notes, it also frees writers up to concoct more creative text.

Because better writing skills lead to higher test scores and better essays, working on handwriting now can benefit your child throughout his school years. Try the following tips to keep your writing practice fun:

* Write a letter to an out-of-town relative together.

* Ask your child to write you a recipe for pancakes before you make them together, or recruit him to help write up your grocery list.

* Paint a particular wall or room in your house with chalkboard or whiteboard paint, creating a space where your child can actually write on the wall.

* Make writing materials easily accessible in his play spaces to promote writing practice during play.

* Draw together and write sentences to describe the pictures.

* Encourage him to write his own story, movie, or play.

Tips to Help Yourself

Feel like there's no way you could possibly hold on to your child's notes from this memory game because your house is already overrun with paper as it is? We're with you. But that's one of the reasons it's great to be parenting in the digital age!

These days there are tons of cool apps for your phone, tablet, and computer that let you take and store pictures of all the amazing stuff your kid churns out on a daily basis. Once you load the images into your account, you can toss the originals in the trash! School art projects celebrating Arbor Day? Snap 'em and trash 'em! A hundred and eighty-five pieces of construction paper covered in stickers of dogs wearing clothes? Snap 'em and trash 'em! The first time your kid writes his own name? Well, you might want to keep that one for posterity. But the *second* through the *fiftieth*? Snap 'em and trash 'em!

Some of the programs are even set up to automatically share all your photos with friends and relatives. So if the grandparents can't take a trip to see your pocket-sized Picasso's works of art every week, you can send your new clutter-free gallery to them!

The Sweet, Sticky Squish of Success

This is it.

The experiment you've been waiting for.

The one that will tell you once and for all whether your child is destined for greatness or destined to crash on your couch for extended periods of her adult life.

But no pressure or anything.

Perform this classic "marshmallow test" on your tiny tyke to find out if she has what scientists believe it takes to truly make it big. Or if that's too intimidating for you, just use it as an excuse to eat a whole bunch of marshmallows. (We're not judging.)

Age	Abilities Tested
4–5 years	Goal Setting, Self-control

What You Need

- ☞ a table and chair
- ☞ a boring, distraction-free room containing the table and chair and ideally not much else (think formal dining room or empty workplace conference room types of settings)
- ☞ 2 identical marshmallows or other small treats your kid would be interested in eating
- ☞ a hidden video camera or video baby monitor so you can watch your child's behavior during the experiment from another room

How It Works

1. Sit your child down at the table and place one of the marshmallows on the table right in front of her.

2. Tell her you need to leave the room but that you're going to keep this marshmallow right here. Explain that if she stays in her seat and doesn't eat the treat while you are gone, then she will get *two* marshmallows to eat when you come back!

3. Leave the room for about 15 minutes. While you're gone, record your child's behavior with a hidden video camera, watch her using a hidden video baby monitor, or at least peek at her through a window so you can see what she does.

4. End the experiment by doing one of the following:

   * If your child eats the marshmallow before you come back, do not give her the second treat.

   * If your child gives up by leaving the room or throwing an epic tantrum to get you to come back, you can let her eat the first treat but not the second.

   * If your child does not eat the treat or give up for approximately 15 minutes, return and reward her with *both* treats.

If the field of developmental psychology ever put out a "greatest hits" album, this simple experiment would undoubtedly be Track Number One. Ever since some researchers at Stanford University first came up with this little beauty back in the late 1960s, it's not only been referenced by scientists and academics galore, but it's also made its way into popular culture by way of movies, music, and even TV commercials.

We suspect much of the experiment's enduring popularity actually stems from the fact that it's absolutely adorable to watch kids try to control themselves with a big, mouth-watering, infinitely tempting treat right in front of their chubby little cheeks. But it also might have something to do with the fact that the results of this experiment have been shown to predict children's future success—all the way into adulthood.

So about that—how did your child do?

Did she gobble up the marshmallow before you even had a chance to close the door behind you, or did she actually wait the entire, excruciatingly long period of time you were gone? If she did wait, you may have observed her trying to distract herself in a number of delightful ways. She might have closed her eyes so she didn't have to see the marshmallow. She could have sung, swung her legs, or talked to herself to take her mind off the situation. Or she may have even touched the marshmallow with her tongue as if to temporarily sate herself until she could eventually suck down all of its sugary goodness for real. These behaviors are not just hilariously cute to watch—they also represent useful distraction techniques that may have helped your child succeed.

This experiment requires your child to keep a goal in mind and to exercise intense, sustained willpower to achieve it. These are the same skills that are needed to achieve all kinds of major life goals. Like working hard to do well in school for the eventual reward of getting into a good college. Or regularly buckling down to practice a musical instrument with the goal of one day mastering it. Or avoiding daily diet-busting temptations to ultimately achieve weight loss.

So if your child *did* wait, it points to great things for her future. The fact that she was able to exert willpower to reach a goal in this situation suggests she has the skills to do it in real life, too. Researchers have conducted this experiment on young children and followed them for decades to see how they turned out. The results showed that children's success in this task predicted all sorts of better outcomes, including higher SAT scores and lower levels of obesity.

Which means this experiment is probably the only time anybody ever *doubled their marshmallow intake* to stay in shape!

Tips to Help Your Child

Did your kid give in and eat the marshmallow, and now you're freaking out because you're pretty sure she'll never make anything of herself? First of all, try to relax and take a few deep breaths. (If you can't take any deep breaths because you completely stuffed your *own* mouth with marshmallows as soon as you started stressing out about all this, at least we now know where your kid gets it.) Seriously though, it's not the end of the world. It turns out that there are lots of ways you can help your impatient imp improve her goal-setting and gratification-delaying skills. Here are some good ones:

* *Set limits and lovingly enforce them.* Learning to follow rules in everyday situations teaches your child self-control. That's a big reason why kids from households with clear and consistent rules tend to perform better on tests like this one. So don't be a wuss when it's time to lay the smackdown on things like bedtimes, eating vegetables, and not jumping on siblings' faces. But don't exert *too much* control over your child's behavior either, as it can hamper her ability to become a confident and independent member of society. Aim to balance strong household rules with lots of love and encouragement. Your child should know what is expected of her and feel supported in reaching your family's goals for behavior.

* *Be proactive.* You can help your child by trying to anticipate possible barriers to her success. Researchers conducted a delay-of-gratification test in which toddlers had to resist touching an

attractive-looking present. The kids were much more successful when their parents anticipated they would have difficulty
with the task and used distraction techniques to divert their
attention away from the present. You can do the same thing for
your child in real-life situations. For example, prevent potential
problems doing homework by designating a quiet workspace
for your child and carving out dedicated time during the day
for her to complete it.

* ***Be a good model.*** Kids are highly influenced by the behavior
they observe in others. In experiments like this one, children
who watched other people exert self-control to effectively wait
for a reward were more likely to wait themselves, while children who watched people failing to wait and favoring immediate gratification were more likely to fail as well. So exercise
the strong influence you have on your child by modeling good
delay-of-gratification skills yourself. For example, instead of
maxing out your credit cards to put a brand-new big screen in
the living room the day it comes out, you can save a little each
month until you have enough to pay for it with cash—and be
sure to share this goal-setting strategy with your kid, too!

* ***Communicate and refocus.*** If you ever sense your child is
beginning to give up on her goals, help her stay on course by
reminding her what she's working so hard to achieve. "Remember that if you get all of your spelling words right, you'll get a
really cool sticker on your test paper!" or "I know you don't
want to pick up your room, Sweetie, but if you stop now, we're
never going to find the cat." A few supportive words from you
may be all she needs to stay motivated.

Tips to Help Yourself

Another reason not to take your child's performance too seriously is
that *you* may have screwed up the experiment. We're not just talking

about the normal ways you might mess up these tests—setting things up incorrectly, getting so excited or nervous about the results that you forget a critical step, neglecting to ensure your younger child is well enough occupied that he doesn't invade in the middle of the experiment and blow it to smithereens. (Can you tell that we've flubbed up our fair share of experiments, too?)

We're actually referring to the effect your past interactions may have unwittingly had on your child's performance. If you've been reliable in fulfilling promises made to your kid in the past, she'll be more likely to wait for the reward when you offer it. But if your kid feels like you've *made* a lot more promises than you've *kept* over the years, she may decide it's not actually worth the wait—and that even though the immediate reward is smaller, she should get her sugar fix now, while the getting's good.

You can avoid this potential bias during the experiment by having someone your child is less familiar with—like one of your coworkers, friends, or third cousins once removed—be the person who promises the marshmallows. But if you did the experiment yourself, it's possible your child's results actually say more about you than they do about your child.

Being trustworthy is essential for creating a good relationship with your child. If you promise her a trip to the park, accept the fact that there are swing sets and slides in your immediate future. If you tell her she can have ice cream for dessert, get ready to spoon over the good stuff. You might figure your child is just a little kid who needs to learn to deal with disappointment if something else comes up or if you happen to change your mind. But remember that she takes your word extremely seriously, so all those little disappointments can lead to some big-time disillusionment if you aren't careful.

Your child may still be tiny, but she's a fully formed human being full of hopes, dreams, and emotions. Show her the respect she deserves, and she'll show you everything she's capable of in life.

Imagine That!

I f that last experiment is still sticking in your craw, we've got good news for you—marshmallows aren't the only test in town.

Although it's true that exhibiting self-control can predict awesome achievements for lots of kids, there are plenty of successful adults who went through childhood with overactive imaginations, insatiable sweet tooths, and a general inability to sit still.

This experiment shows you a clever way to evaluate your kid's current *creative* abilities and then use *them* to forecast his future chance at success!

Age	Ability Tested
4 years and older	Creativity

What You Need

☞ a spoon

☞ a stuffed animal

☞ a set of incomplete picture fragments like the ones shown here

☞ some crayons, markers, or colored pencils

How It Works

This experiment is actually three experiments in one! Each phase below is completely independent of the other two, so you can do them in any order, and at any times, that you want.

☛ **PART 1**

1. Hand your child a spoon and ask him to think of as many uses as he can for it.

2. Encourage him to keep coming up with new ideas for as long as he can.

☛ **PART 2**

1. Show your child a stuffed animal and ask him, "How would you make this a better toy? What would you do to it to make it more fun?" (Don't worry at all if the improvements he suggests aren't actually possible.)

2. Next ask him, "Can you think of any ways to use this besides just playing with it?"

3. Encourage him to keep generating answers to both questions for as long as he can.

☛ **PART 3**

1. Using a full sheet of paper, redraw the six squares with line fragments in them shown on the previous page. It's OK if your drawings don't look exactly like these—any old line fragment will do.

2. Give your child the crayons, markers, or pencils, and ask him to use the line fragments to complete a picture.

If these experiments feel like simple, fun games to play with your child, that's because they are! But they're also enlightening ways to test your child's creativity skills. For each of the tests, you'll want to analyze your kid's responses according to the following criteria:

* **Number of relevant responses.** How many ideas did your child generate? The more distinct responses he gave that were truly related to the question, the more it indicates good creativity skills. Plus there's a relationship between the number of answers people produce in response to a question and the quality of the ideas—with *later* responses tending to be more creative. So it's a good sign if your kid can keep those ideas coming!

* **Uniqueness of responses.** Were your child's responses typical (like using the spoon to eat soup) or more inventive (like using the spoon for a hot tub at a fairy pool party)? In the drawing task, kids show uniqueness of their responses through less straightforward uses of the lines (like using a curved line as the start of a ring around a planet in an elaborate outer space scene instead of as the mouth of a simple smiley face). Breaking boundaries, drawing outside of squares, and other unusual uses of the drawing space should be considered very creative too! Kids also get extra creativity points for any answers that are humorous, ironic, or emotionally expressive.

* **Level of detail.** How much did he elaborate on his responses? After hearing him describe his idea for turning the stuffed animal into a teddy bear time machine, do you feel like you have enough information to draw up the blueprints right now? Your child shows more creativity when he gives you *lots* of imaginative details. Abstract, fictional, and other made-up features also indicate good creativity skills.

The same scoring scheme can be used to assess creativity at any age, from preschool all the way through adulthood. But creativity does appear to change over time. For example, in the picture task, very young kids may initially draw pictures inside the boxes that do not even incorporate the line fragments. As they get older, they may begin *copying* the line fragments, then *closing* them to make simple shapes, until ultimately they develop the ability to use the fragments in more complex and creative pictures. Some research suggests that kids' creativity in these kinds of tasks increases until it peaks in the elementary school years, dropping off in later school years and adulthood. Andy's informal, historical, and very *personal* research indicates that by around age twelve, boys can turn *any* line fragment you give them into a picture of boobs.

Any. Line. Fragment.

Although creativity changes with age, the *relative* amount of creativity a person shows compared to their peers stays fairly consistent throughout life. For that reason, if your adolescent artiste shows high levels of creativity right now, there's a good chance he'll maintain his imaginative behavior into adulthood. It's true! Researchers administered a creativity test to elementary school children that included questions similar to the ones in this experiment. When they followed up with the same kids forty years later, they found that adults who were more creative as children were more likely to have become successful in creative pursuits like music, art, drama, and literature.

Tips to Help Your Child

Want to help your kid's creativity really shine? Here are some ways to foster a creative home environment that can help your child hone his skills:

* *Play!* Research shows that children's play skills are a sign of their budding creativity skills. So cultivate a habit of play and

exploration, no matter what you're doing. Approach everything with a sense of fun and curiosity, from playing at the
park to exploring a new science concept.

✳ *Have some laughs.* Humor can promote creativity. One
research study tested children's creativity skills after some of
the kids had listened to a funny recording and others had not.
The ones who listened to knock-knock jokes knocked the test
out of the park! So keep things light at home, and your child
could end up with some heavy creativity skills.

✳ *Use open-ended toys.* Playtime materials like paper and markers, play dough, and blocks don't have a fixed use like many
other kids' toys. The only limit to how these materials can be
used is your child's imagination. So make these open-ended
materials available, encourage your child to use them, and
watch his creativity flourish.

✳ *Play the picture completion game.* The drawing task used
in this experiment can be a regular game you play with your
child. Just draw any line you want and challenge your child to
turn it into a picture. It makes drawing a fun, interactive game
and helps kids practice their creativity skills. In fact, any of
these creativity tests can be made into everyday games!

✳ *Follow the creativity guidelines.* Now that you have some
concrete criteria for measuring creativity (number of relevant responses, uniqueness of responses, and level of detail),
use them to promote creativity at home. Practice generating
multiple solutions to everyday problems by exhausting many
possibilities before settling on one. Model creative behavior
by trying to come up with unique responses and lots of detail
yourself, and encourage your child to do the same.

Tips to Help Yourself

As we're sure you know by now, being a parent is a nonstop, stamina-sucking grind. That's why we saved our best tip for last:

Take a break!

Even though there's always some hand-holding, mess cleaning, and wisdom imparting you *could* be doing for your kid, sometimes the best gift you can give him is to just do *nothing*. When you resist the urge to constantly teach your child everything every single minute of the day, he'll be free to explore and learn about the world on his own—which can boost his creativity big time.

Not buying it yet? Here's an example for you.

Multiple research studies have examined how kids behave after an adult gives them a new toy. Some kids were explicitly taught how the toy worked, while others received the toy without any instruction. The children who were formally taught about the toy showed more limited play, using the toy in only those ways that were demonstrated. But the lucky little kiddos who were not formally taught about the toy showed more diverse and creative play, discovering additional new features of the toy all on their own.

You know what we call that?

Fun.

And despite all the work you want to do to ensure your child's success in the future, *fun* will always be the best measure of your child's success *right now*.

Give that to him, and you can give yourself a well-deserved pat on the back.

Nice work, Mom and Dad.

Keep it up.

Final Thoughts

●●●●●●●●●●●●●●●●●●●●●●●●●●●●●●●●●●●●●●●

At the beginning of this book, we were dealing with a clueless, helpless, constantly bewildered human being just trying to make sense of the world.

You.

Thankfully by now, you're probably way more comfortable with this whole parenting thing than you used to be. Our hope is that the experiments we presented here have played at least some small role in that. Some of them clued you in to your child's impressive mental prowess, while others let you witness your kid's increasing social skills. They've shown you that there were times when your kid knew a lot more—or a lot less—than you may have thought.

Taken as a whole, these experiments helped you see how your child's seemingly unpredictable flurry of disconnected behavior is actually all related. Once you learned how to uncover patterns in your kid's thinking, you were better able to make sense of it, withstand it, appreciate it, exploit it, and most importantly—promote it. Because you have taken the time to observe, interact with, and really think about your child's development while reading this book, there's a great chance you've just improved your *own* development as a parent.

And that's the best result any experiment could hope for.

Best of luck to you. Happy parenting, and keep on experimenting!

Acknowledgments

* *

To our kids, Sammy and Freddy, thank you for filling our lives with laughter and love, teaching us everything we truly know about parenting, and giving us a reason to write this book.

To Andy's parents, Mary Jo and Jim Ankowski, thank you for your support, enthusiasm, and the empty journal to fill up with our ideas. To Amber's parents, Karen and Jack Aguiar, thank you for giving us the love, encouragement, and babysitting we needed so we actually had time to write them all down!

To our original test subject, Abigail Cummings, thank you for having such a cute and hilarious reaction to a cookie-breaking experiment that it inspired this entire book. To Heather and Steve Udell and Kristin and Terry Davies, thank you for letting us frequently experiment on our adorable little nieces. To Heather and Jason Aguiar, thank you for your constant support of our creative pursuits. To Nicole and Rob Harvilla, thank you for your insight, imagination, and enthusiasm, and for telling us we really *should* do this.

To our friends Jen and Abhijay Prakash, thank you for believing in us and insisting we write a book in the first place, and to Ashleigh and TJ Sochor, Ali Barker, Megan Baltruzak, Dave Cooper, Erica Srinivasan, and Barry and Marla Schwartz, thank you for generously giving your time, expertise, and friendship to help make what we wrote better.

To Amber's professional colleagues and friends who have played a part in the making of this book, especially Emily Russell, Virginia Huynh, Ji Son, Haley Vlach, Mariel Kyger, and Elizabeth Darvick, thank you for being a constant source of support and inspiration. To Christia Brown, thank you for helping us navigate the publication process. To mentors Cathy Sandhofer, Aaron Blaisdell, Scott Johnson, and Patricia Greenfield, thank you for teaching Amber to become a competent enough researcher to write this book.

To our agent, Uwe Stender, whose enthusiasm for us and our work has never faltered, and to Lisa Reardon and the entire staff at Chicago Review Press, thank you for working with us to bring this book to life!

References

·······································

L ooking for some additional "light reading" on the subject of child development? See below for a few of the most accessible and commercially available resources we referenced while writing this book. If you're interested in reading the entire, massive list of highly technical research articles that support our experimental methods and factual statements, please check out our website at www.doctoranddad.com.

Bronson, Po, and Ashley Merryman. 2009. *NurtureShock: New Think ing About Children*. New York: Twelve.

Eliot, Lise. 1999. *What's Going on in There?: How the Brain and Mind Develop in the First Five Years of Life*. New York: Bantam Books.

Faber, Adele, and Elaine Mazlish. 2002. *How to Talk So Kids Will Listen & Listen So Kids Will Talk*. New York: Harper Collins.

Hoff, Erika. 2009. *Language Development*. Belmont, CA: Wadsworth.

Lightfoot, Cynthia, Michael Cole, and Sheila R. Cole. 2005. *The Development of Children*. New York: Worth Publishers.

Newman, Barbara M., and Philip R. Newman. 2009. *Development Through Life: A Psychosocial Approach*. Belmont, CA: Wadsworth Cengage Learning.

Siegler, Robert S., and Martha Wagner Alibali. 2005. *Children's Thinking*. Upper Saddle River, NJ: Pearson Prentice Hall.

Index

About the Authors

Amber Ankowski earned her PhD in developmental psychology from the University of California, Los Angeles. Her articles have been published in the academic journals *Child Development Research*, *Infant and Child Development*, and *Journal of Experimental Psychology*. She teaches psychology at various California universities, including courses designed to instruct future educators how best to teach young children. **Andy Ankowski** studied creative writing while obtaining his BA in English at the University of Notre Dame. He is an award-winning advertising copywriter and creative director who specializes in explaining complex products and services in simple and humorous ways. Together, they are the parents of two children, whom they teach and learn from every day.